PTSD – Cleaning and Clearing Shock & Trauma

FINDING FREEDOM

by

STEPHEN P. KING

This book is dedicated to all of my clients that have honoured me with their sharing, their sensitivity, insights, wounds, wisdom and willingness to be open to fresh possibility and processing and make the move from being survivors to becoming tenacious thrivers.

Published - Penticton, B.C., Canada - May 2016.

Copyright 2016 Stephen P. King. All rights reserved.
ISBN 978-0-9950865-0-0

No part of this publication may be reproduced, stored in a retrieval system, or transmitted, in any form or by any means, electronic, mechanical, photocopying, recording, or otherwise, without the written permission of the author.

CONTENTS

ABOUT the AUTHOR

Stephen (Steve) King has a B.Sc. degree in Health and Human Services and is a Registered Clinical Counsellor. He is an avid runner, race-walker and triathlete who has held six national age group records, has raced at Ironman and Ultraman triathlon distances and has been a member of Canada`s national 100km team. In 2001 he became the second Canadian ever to complete the grueling Badwater Death Valley 135 mile run and he put together a a photo journal of this challenge on YouTube, accompanied by the song 'Road to Hell' (written by Rea/Anton) and sung by Steve himself. https://www.youtube.com/watch?v=GZFEMIsydFA Steve was also the publisher of `Tri-Fit Quarterly`, a national triathlon magazine, author of a triathlon training log and CBC`s color commentator for triathlon. He is also the race announcer for many sports events including Ironman Canada (now Challenge Penticton). He has an avid interest in healthy balance and wholism and in 2012 he was inducted into the BC Athletics Hall of Fame and was honored by a local couple of businessmen who recently produced a bobblehead likeness of Steve, which even has its own Facebook page of photos showing him bobbing up in a variety of locales around the world (Adventures of #bobblehead Steve). Steve has worked at Pathways Addictions Resource Centre in Penticton since 1989 and he authored a book on energy psychology entitled, `*Rapid Recovery: Accelerated Information Processing & Healing*` http://bookstore.trafford.com/Products/SKU-000154875/Rapid-Recovery.aspx and co-edited '*Running in the Zone*` and is a contributing writer to '*Gin & Platonic and Other Short Stories with a Twist'* and '*Triathlete in Transition'*. Steve also recorded a 16-song CD dedicated to his wife Jean entitled 'Songs for Jean', which can be heard by visiting http://www.cdbaby.com/cd/steveking1 Additional information can be found on Steve's website at http://www2.vip.net/~stking/

N.B. Stephen (Steve) King's companion PTSD online video course can be previewed at https://www.udemy.com/post-traumatic-stress-disorder/?instructorPreviewMode=guest

Target Readership

"My message is always the same: to cultivate and practice love, kindness, compassion and tolerance." - Dalai Lama

This book has been written for use by and for the benefit of the following:

Professionals:
- Counsellors
- Clinicians
- Therapists
- Critical Incident Stress Debriefers
- Psychologists
- Psychiatrists
- Mental Health Practitioners
- Trauma specialists
- Students of Psychology/Psychiatry/Criminology

Clients and patients of the above including:

- Military veterans
- Victims of crime or abuse
- Victims of terror
- Those who suffer from trauma and shock
- Sufferers who have not sought treatment
- Sufferers who are getting treatment but have not yet been successful in processing their traumatic histories.

- Those who have repeated nightmares or images that haunt them.
- Those who have had emotional, sexual or physical trauma from accidents or deliberate acts of violence or have been witness to same.
- Those who have had vicarious trauma.
- Those who have been 'uncomfortably spotlighted' – which could include having been bullied.
- Those with 'stuck/frozen' memories/images.
- Loved ones who wish to share new possibilities with victims of shock and trauma

No doubt that many of you will be skeptical about some of the contents of this course and I urge you to honour that - but what I request in return is that you please "Humour me!" and see how things unfold.

What matters in the end is - did it work?

"Effectiveness is the measure of truth." (Huna tenet)

Safety & Disclaimer

"If we don't change, we don't grow. If we don't grow, we are not really living. Growth demands a temporary surrender of security." Gail Sheehy

A great deal of importance has to be given to the issue of safety and support, just as one would if providing therapy or being the recipient of same.

To this end, I have to make a disclaimer that any professional using these techniques must do so with the express understanding that compliance with their respective professional governing body's code of ethics must be adhered to in all respects - and that those who may choose to utilise these tools and techniques directly for themselves, do so with the following recommendations.

If you attend any support group such as AA/NA etc. that if you have a sponsor whom you are very comfortable with – that you request their support and permission to contact, if required, for any debriefing you may need as a result.

If you are a member of any Mental Health group or have a personal, professional counsellor/therapist – that you inform them of what you will be doing and request their support and permission to contact, if required, for any debriefing you may need as a result.

Having a friend or family member you can call upon, if required. Please let at least one know in advance that you might be contacting them for debriefing purposes.

Inform any of the above of the journey you are about to undertake. It is not necessary to provide them with any details of the trauma/shock – that is for you to decide. However, I would urge you to confirm that you can call or request support if necessary.

One final safety issue.

Be aware that cleaning and clearing one memory may allow or cause another or others to surface – the same techniques can be applied but, if it is not an appropriate time or place in which to do so, use some inner dialogue (thanking the self for the information and awareness) to acknowledge that, but that it presently needs to be safely retained until conditions can provide you with the time and the environment in which to process same.

CHAPTER ONE

What is Healing?

"The quintessential possibility of regressive therapy is spiritual opening and the emergence of a volitional relationship with one's higher Self." (Emerson p. 28)

In order to establish exactly what healing means, it is necessary to understand the basic human needs and the multi-faceted nature of the wounds that can afflict us.

Charles Whitfield has developed a more thorough list of the hierarchy of human needs than the oft-quoted Maslow's list, and it's based on the work of a number of researchers (Maslow, 1962; Miller, 1981; Weil, 1973; Glasser, 1985).

- Survival
- Safety
- Touching, skin contact
- Attention
- Mirroring and echoing
- Guidance
- Listening
- Being real

- Participating

- Acceptance: i.e. Others are aware of and take seriously and admire the Real You -

  Freedom to be the Real You - Tolerance of your feelings - Validation

  Respect - Belonging and love.

- Opportunity to grieve losses and to grow
- Support
- Loyalty and trust
- Accomplishment: i.e., Mastery - Power - Control - Creativity -

  Having a sense of completion - Making a contribution.

- Altering one's state of consciousness, transcending the ordinary.
- Sexuality
- Enjoyment or fun
- Freedom
- Nurturing
- Unconditional love (including connection with a Higher Power)   (Whitfield p. 18)

If this unified model is recognized as being acceptable for understanding our personal needs, it becomes quite apparent that very few people would get all of these needs met in their childhood. Parents or significant adults may not have the knowledge, tools, or wherewithal to accommodate these needs in the best of circumstances. If there were abuses or traumas that were never fully and healthily attended to in the formative years, then it likely falls to the individual to resolve the issues. The most devastating result of childhood abuse and trauma is the loss of the 'true' self. The major goal for many can therefore be viewed as attaining a state of unconditional Self-acceptance.

Even if one were to arrive at such a healthy state of being, the more left-brained amongst us would want to know, before undertaking the journey, just what that might look and feel like. Some of the signs of inner peace are:

- Tendency to think and act spontaneously rather than from fear based on past experiences.
- An unmistakable ability to enjoy each moment.
- Loss of interest in judging other people.
- Loss of interest in judging self.
- Loss of interest in interpreting the actions of others.
- Loss of interest in conflict.
- Loss of ability to worry (a very serious symptom)

- Frequent, overwhelming episodes of appreciation.

- Contented feelings of connectedness with nature and others.

- Frequent attacks of smiling through the eyes from the heart.

- Increased tendency to let things happen rather than make them happen.

- Increased susceptibility to Love extended by others, as well as the uncontrollable urge to extend it.

(*Olympia Fellowship of Reconciliation Newsletter.* I.63, 1986)

Both Scott Peck and Dr. Bernie Siegel have suggested that we are born with a belief that we deserve to be loved. This makes a lot of sense to me as we have to question why it would be that we would have low self-esteem or emotional turmoil 'simply' because we lived in a non-welcoming environment – after all what's to lose or feel bad about if there were no preconceived expectation?

Joan Borysenko wrote about a documentary on Mother Teresa and her visit to a home for spastic children in Lebanon in which the children appeared small for their ages and of stunted stature.

They were suffering from an illness known as hospitalism, or
failure to thrive, that occurs often in group homes for infants.
Although the children are fed and changed their needs are
met on schedule with little chance for the give and take that is
natural between infant and caretaker. The pituitary glands of
these unloved children fail to put out enough growth
hormone. In effect, the baby gives itself a die message since
there is no one to receive. (p. 17)

Others, such as Stanislav Grof, Arthur Janov, and Dr. William
Emerson have provided evidence which demonstrates that
pre-birth trauma can create a life-long negative impact. It can
be like 'acid rain on one's soul'.

A Mother is able, via hormones carried in the blood, to
transmit emotions through the umbilical cord to her fetus.
Because they are present in the ever-changing composition of
the amniotic fluid, the fetus is literally "marinating" in any
stressors taking place in its family or environment during the
prenatal period.

There are few people who would suggest that they have an
alcohol problem as a result of excessive thirst! In fact, as with
most addictive behaviors, clients tend to recognize that they

use mood-altering substances or processes for exactly that reason - to alter their mood or the way they feel.

The first three items of the Suicide Status Form (SSF) that was derived from a theoretical model presented by E. S. Schneidman (*Definition of Suicide*. New York: Wiley. 1985) were pain, press, and perturbation. Schneidman's model of suicide conceptualizes the acute suicidal moment as a convergence of these three major dimensions. Psychic *pain* is defined as an unbearable level of psychological suffering, *press* relates to pressures (stressors) that impinge on one's psychological world, and *perturbation* is a general term describing an intense state of emotional upset, and is thought to include agitation, perceptual constriction, impulsiveness, and a penchant for action. The action is the distraction!

The three things that seem to be underlying the feelings of stress are:

1. Fear. 2. Pain. 3. Fear of more pain.
It is necessary to also recognize that fear and pain are not just felt in the physical form, but also in the emotional. This therefore impacts the psyche and our spirit. It is not surprising therefore that, in the 90's, addiction was being recognized as having biopsychosocial components. Much emphasis is also

placed on "Spirituality" in the healing process of addictions, especially for those in 12-step programs, and it often creates some confusion for newcomers who are told or believe that spirituality and religion are synonymous. It has been said to me that, "Religion is for people trying to stay out of hell - Spirituality is for people who have already been there."

For those who have had unpleasant experiences with the issue of religion, this can, of course, create problems and severely hinder their willingness or ability to move forward in the healing process. However, I believe that if we are born with automatic personal survival skills (fight or flight, dissociation etc.) that some would say are God-given or Higher Power driven, then it seems reasonable to expect that the same God or Higher Power would also provide us with self-autonomous ways to resolve those same traumas.

I believe that the herein-described Accelerated Information Processing techniques (AIP's) are a part of that self-autonomy equation.

Any true goal-setting needs to be SMART, i.e. **S**pecific, **M**easurable, **A**greeable, **R**ealistic and **T**ime-sensitive. The AIP's described herein fit well with this goal-setting model.

Pain can be a manifestation of repressed subconscious emotions such as anger, fear, or sorrow, say a number of experts. Root out and face those feelings and you should be able to say farewell to psychogenic distress (pain that originates in the psyche and manifests itself in the body). The key is acceptance. Gestalt therapy calls the habit of turning powerful emotions inward "retroflexion." Lisbet Trier-Rosner, says that in Gestalt therapy, clients with shoulder pain or chronic stiff tension may be encouraged to hit a pillow hard and repeatedly. This usually releases anger and the armoring of muscles in the shoulders, and it generally helps the person remember what caused the anger. Therapies that are more "hands-on" can sometimes actually work the buried emotion right out of the painful area, because as Toronto chiropractor Paul Truelove says, "The emotion *is* the pain." (*Pathways* Magazine. 'Pain - Healing from the inside out'. P. Ohlendorf-Moffat. pps. 28-33)

Healing can be about putting the ego aside and challenging one's existing paradigms and behaviors. It can be about moving away from being a "stubborn victim" to being a "tenacious survivor". About possibly being willing to move from anal-retentive to expressive. In fact Dr. Dean Ornish refers to his work with heart disease patients as "emotional open-heart surgery." (Moyers p. 69)

If we accept the idea that we are born with a belief that we deserve to be loved and that the hierarchy of needs list is relevant to our personal sense of wellness, then it is appropriate to establish an understanding of the meaning of spirituality and its inevitable connection to our relationship with ourselves, with other people, and with Mother Earth.

I will often demonstrate with my open hand, fully unfolded and palm up, how, if we are born into a healthy family unit or environment and feel loved, wanted, and nurtured, our spirit will remain open and have a sense of belonging in the world. If this continued, one would grow up feeling valued and comfortable in owning and pursuing one's own passions, beliefs, interests - i.e. fully connected to one's own spirit and being comfortable in one's own skin.

Psychologist Alice Miller (*The Untouched Key: Tracing Childhood Trauma in Creativity and Destructiveness*) and many others, have documented the numerous affects of childhood abuse, so it is not much of a leap to recognize that, if one were to be born into an unhealthy family situation or environment, then a sense of unworthiness will start to manifest, only to become further entrenched by ongoing incidents, statements, or traumas, whether directed at the self, or witnessed. This leads a person to feel unworthy, anxious, disconnected, dissociated, depressed and therefore DIS-SPIRITED. This can be demonstrated by slowly closing the open hand. The soul may get sealed shut!

Many people spend a lifetime seeking that 'missing' sense of external acceptance and will try and become whatever they feel they need to, in order to gain acceptance and love by those from whom they desire it. This can result in a constant return to situations and behaviors that might be against one's true beliefs, and are usually against one's own best interests. This will only add to the internalized, and often verbalized, sense of unworthiness and low self-esteem. Having to give up one's true self in order to try and gain love from someone else will often result in so-called co-dependent relationships and a very unfulfilling life -a life of surviving rather than truly living.

This loss of self can be viewed as a form of self-abandonment and, if the emotional or physical pain is too great, then self-rejection and self-hatred can quickly follow. To put it into full context, by our action and thought we have the ability to become our own worst enemy. The addicted person will view the alcohol or drugs as a best friend regardless of the consequences of using. It is interesting to note how the alcoholic or addict can relate to feeling "at one", able to conquer the world, solve issues, be the clown, the entertainer, the masterful orator - yet would feel uncomfortable or unwilling to 'act' in the same way without the substance. The fact that alcohol is also called "spirits" might help us understand that it can be both a bridge and a barrier to the self. Trauma, abuse, and abandonment issues have caused life-long psychological and behavioral scars. Internalized shame, guilt, anger and fears gradually erode the spirit, fuelled by ongoing repetition of negative thoughts and "anticipatory anxiety", which will eventually manifest itself in self-sabotage. The word sabotage comes from the French "sabot", meaning shoe. This was because disgruntled shoe factory workers would sometimes deliberately throw a shoe into the machinery to make it break down. (Whisenant p. 102)

Addictions workers are familiar with the identified family systems roles that individuals in alcohol or drug misuser-affected family members tend to assume or fall into. They fall into categories such as the chemical abuser, the enabler, the family hero, the clown/mascot, the lost child, the scapegoat, the caretaker, and the placator. These are not absolutes or inevitables, but many clients state that they can identify with a particular role and behaviors, as well as fit other family members into some of the other roles.

I have found that there is often another role taken on by one of the children, and that is one that I would call the "Super-sensitive". This appears to happen when no adult family member shows any obvious signs of legitimate shame and/or guilt, so the 'me' or 'true self' gets lost, as that person (the super-sensitive) takes on the family shame, guilt, morality or sense of ethics. The guilt can lead the super-sensitive to feel that they deserve to 'die', in an emotional and/or spiritual sense.

Patterns of negative behavior will continue to re-enact themselves until such time as a person looks at the beliefs, the thinking and the feelings that underlie them, and consciously gives him/herself permission to work through their issues. In other words, "To finish the unfinished business."

Even though the ego is designed to act in your own best interests, it will stunt you from attaining your true full potential as it will jump in and remind you of a similar past situation that resulted in some discomfort/pain. If the original injury is a recent one then this would be very valid, but not if it is based on an "old" childhood wound. If the ego is not provided with new information about our ability as an adult to truly choose our present experiences, then it will step in and block our potential for growth. The self becomes stunted, and this 'freezing/blocking' of the self at an early emotional age is what many experience in their everyday lives. They may biologically be 50 years of age, but when confronted with a present experience that has some similarities to old unfinished business, i.e. an angry adult, then they may feel themselves emotionally revert to feeling and behaving like a terrified ten year-old.

This type of experience can be likened to an emotional near death experience (NDE), add to that some major physical or sexual traumas, and the possibility of post-traumatic-stress-disorder (PTSD) is a reality. PTSD is becoming a common diagnosis for survivors of trauma, rather than being reserved for those who have suffered as a result of war. For a number of people their family or life experiences have contained the same dynamics as that of a war zone.

Many victims will show little or no affect, their feelings or emotions have been frozen. The term "Alexithymia" has been used, mostly for men who have no congruency between what they have experienced and the feelings that would normally be connected to that experience. (*Psychology Today*. 'Men Without Passion'. Dec. 1988. pps. 20-22)

Dr. Richard Gerber explains the most familiar form of Einstein's relativity equation ($E = mc2$) and also the proportionality constant known as the Einstein-Lorentz Transformation. This constant is the relativistic factor that describes how different parameters of measurement will vary according to the velocity of the system being described. Dr. Gerber also describes what he calls the Tiller-Einstein Model (after Dr. William Tiller of Stanford University) which may well explain the phenomena of subtle energies. This model explains both positive and negative space/time. This negative space/time model recognizes negative particles and mass, therefore matter, which would demonstrate the property of negative entropy (the ability to reassemble a disordered system).

The energy contained within a particle is equivalent to the product of its mass multiplied by the speed of light squared. This means that there is an incredible amount of potential energy stored within a tiny particle of matter. (pps. 143-5)

An important consequence of Einstein's relativity is the realization that matter and energy are interchangeable. Mass is nothing but a form of energy. Matter is simply slowed down or crystallized energy. Our bodies are energy. (Brennan p. 24)

Einstein's famous and elegantly simple formula reduces everything in the universe to a single concept - energy, or light. Energy is essentially vibration. Atoms vibrate, cells vibrate, we vibrate, each with a "note" in the "Cosmic Chorus" unique to ourself. (Hills p. 2)

This suggests that true emotion is therefore energy in motion, and that if we are unable to express and release our feelings then the relevant energy gets suppressed, repressed, and turned against the self, or acted out inappropriately. (Janov 1991, p. 71)

All emotions are, in essence, impulses to act, the instant plans for handling life that evolution has instilled in us. The very root of the word *emotion* is *motere*, the Latin verb "to move," plus the prefix "e- "to connote" "move away" suggesting that a tendency to act is implicit in every emotion. (Goleman p. 6)

Emotion, from "e" meaning out and "movere" to remove, is the moving out of energy in the body, or as John Bradshaw says, "Energy in motion." When we feel emotion, then we are "moved" to initiate something, to make a change, to expand ourselves in some way.

"Emotions are the result of consciousness meeting the body." (Judith/Vega 1993, p. 86), and, as Marilyn Ferguson has stated, "Consciousness is not a tool. It is our being." (1980, p. 362) We know that once a piece of information, negative or positive, has been received, there will be an emotional reaction in the body.

People who are good copers are often referred to as *stress-hardy.* Psychologist Suzanne Kobasa has identified three attitudes that sustain such individuals during demanding times. These attitudes are called the three C's: challenge, commitment, and control. A stress-hardy person sees change and crisis as a challenge rather than a threat. Even when they cannot control the outer situation, they realize that they always have control over their response to the things that are happening. There is a wise saying that relates to this phenomenon: "Suffering is inevitable, but misery is optional." (Cousins p. 26)

It is said that, "what we repress we obsess" and that we turn to action that is designed to act as a distraction. These actions are oftentimes behaviors that are addictive, obsessive, or compulsive. This repression can be consciously or unconsciously fueled by our fears and pain, and will lead to the "psychic numbing" and dissociation that will occur when our basic survival mechanism is triggered to react. With sufficient exposure to traumatic experiences the ego can shatter to the point that mild dissociative experiences can turn into the extreme dissociative experience of multiple personality disorder (now called Dissociative Identity Disorder), in which totally different brain waves have been recorded for different "parts" sharing the same physical body. (Talbot p. 76)

Grief is a legitimate feeling for any change or loss. Part of the resolution of the grieving process is in the acceptance and release of the feeling of anger. Acknowledging that basically anger is just "hurt covered up" can allow us to give ourselves permission to confront it in a healthy way, both physically and emotionally.

If a person grew up in an environment whereby anger was not allowed to be expressed or, if it was expressed in such a way that it meant violence, humiliation, or ridicule, then it becomes understandable why a person might resolve to repress it as a way to avoid owning the feeling, or putting it aside. Fear of one's anger can result in the energy of that emotion eating away on the inside, tying the stomach in knots, turning to rage and having a person end up being "beside him/herself", i.e. dis-connected.

If we accept the premise that a Higher Power provided us with the original ability to feel and express emotions, then we can understand that, when something disturbing happens in a healthy family, the appropriate feelings can get healthily expressed, the matter is dealt with and one returns to a state of homeostasis (balance). If, however, unhealthy expression or repression is role-modelled for us, then when we are thrown out of balance, we will never return to an emotionally healthy status quo, but will go through our lives getting further out of balance and out of touch with our real selves i.e. dis-connected / dis-spirited. "When the connections between the Higher Self and the physical personality become interrupted or blocked, egocentrism, alienation, and feelings of separation occur." (Gerber 1988, p. 281)

It was Dr. Norman Cousins who wrote that; "Death is not the ultimate tragedy of life. The ultimate tragedy is depersonalization – dying in an alien and sterile area, separated from the spiritual nourishment that comes from being able to reach out to a loving hand, separated from a desire to experience the things that make life worth living, separated from hope." (p. 133)

The healing process can begin the moment a person comes out of denial, gives oneself permission to challenge a belief system that just hasn't worked, and allows oneself to slowly begin a process of owning and safely releasing the legitimate feelings that are connected to past experiences. This allows for the dissipation of repressed energy that has been either internalized and is eating away at the self, or has been inappropriately expressed and is negatively impacting one's welfare.

I leave an acronym (AGE) on a board in my office that many clients have referred to and identified with, as it contains a simple truth. **A**buse imprisons, **G**rief releases, and **E**xpression heals.

Healing then is a process of shifting our beliefs, thoughts and actions from that of being "our own worst enemy" into becoming "our own best friend", or at least treating ourselves with the same kindly consideration that we would extend to someone we loved unconditionally. I will sometimes state to a client that, "You are the only person you will never leave or lose in your entire lifetime, so you might as well establish the best possible relationship with yourself." Indeed, congruency and confluence equals mental health.

Truly one is in the high-road harmonious state when living by **THE GOLDEN RULE!**

Childhood or other life experiences can leave a person in a state whereby survival, preservation and dependence are the guiding principles. A state of hopelessness and helplessness will often result in, what Emerson termed "endogeneous depression." Adulthood, however, should be a time of movement toward independence and truly living.

Naturally, we do not want this process of change to take a lifetime, even though we may recognize that "happiness is in the journey and not a destination." It is because the Callahan Technique (TFT) and other Accelerated Information Processing (AIP's) techniques have provided many of my clients with such healthy shifts in a very brief time period that I wish to further an understanding, as well as develop the practice of the same. If we continue to re-enact unhealthy behaviors as a result of not resolving our unfinished business (Emerson 1993, p. 33), then in essence we need an "emotional enema" - a very threatening idea if you believe that pain never ends! Bill Moyers used the analogy of "emotional open heart surgery" (1993, p. 69) for the same concept.

The Hunas recognize the role of *Ku* (subconscious) memory, which resides at the cellular level and does its best to avoid what is painful. The kahunas concept of a *ku* connotes a hidden part of the mind that could also be a reservoir for unresolved conflicts. It is animalistic in the sense that it is directly linked to the functioning of the body and it serves to channel instincts and emotions. However, in the kahuna view *ku* doesn't have to be controlled, only taught or trained. The *ku* is the reservoir not only of unresolved conflicts, but of all learning and habits, and its instinctive drives have to do with survival, growth, and happiness. All the negative effects produced by the *ku* are considered as the result of learned behavior and beliefs. (King 1985, p. 25)

We cannot always control what happens to us or around us, but we can learn to change our responses to those things. We can lead a life in pursuit of our own goals, allowing ourselves the gift of being open to pursue our own true potential and returning to a state of full connectedness with our own spirit. "To lose one's soul eliminates meaning from life." (Achterberg p. 17)

From the "soul murder" that derives from excessive and persistent shame and guilt can come the re-birth and relationship with the self, and the world that offers a sense of real choice and the healthy pursuit of optimum potential and possibilities. Dr. Wayne Dyer has made a significant contribution to the spiritual search that many are journeying on with his book *Your Sacred Self*. He speaks to the fears and doubts that continue to stop one's spiritual growth and states that "Everything you do produces a result. It is what you do with the result that counts." (1995, p. 105). In other words, there is no such thing as failure - only feedback!

If a person could accept all of their natural feelings and moods and develop healthy forms of expressing them, then there would be no need for mood-altering substances or processes. The elimination of fears, phobias, addictions, obsessions, compulsions, and traumas by dissipating the energy of the resulting and underlying anxiety is what appears to happen as a result of using Dr. Callahan's Thought Field Therapy and other AIP's.

It is rare that the term cure is used in the field of psychology, but Dr. Callahan does use the term cure, and the results of his technique appear to have borne this out.

There are a number of definitions for the word *cure* and they include:

- Something that corrects, heals, or permanently alleviates a harmful or troublesome situation.
- To restore to health.
- To free from something objectionable or harmful.

- To rectify an unhealthy or undesirable condition.
- To relieve or be rid of something troublesome or detrimental such as illness, a bad habit, etc.

I have had numerous clients inform me that their original identified problem issues have not returned and therefore, given the elapsed amount of time, I believe the TFT and other AIP treatments can indeed provide a "cure."

It is also a good idea to remember that we have never walked in another person's shoes, and it therefore behooves us to look at the world through another's lens, rather than to be restricted by our own limited experience and views. Otherwise our judgments or reactions become biased and inflexible.

It is a therapist's or counselor's role to support and guide clients towards their stated goals and, in order to do so effectively one occasionally needs to suspend one's beliefs in order to work with and support another through their issues and dilemmas. It was Dr. Schweitzer who said, "The witch doctor succeeds for the same reason all the rest of us succeed. Each patient carries his own doctor inside him. They come to us not knowing that truth. We are at our best when we give the doctor who resides within each patient a chance to go to work." (Cousins p. 69)

The doctor inside that Schweitzer refers to has the benefit of the body's innate wisdom, as well as the life experiences and knowledge that has produced the wisdom of the psyche. I will often ask clients to tune-in to their "independent, expert, observer part", and few ever question what it is I'm asking of them, though many may realize that in order to hear that part they may have to emotionally step aside. Some will feel an internal conflict, and this is often the recognition of some form of secondary gain that is to be had by not listening in too deeply to that part, as it may involve some level of discomfort - some people are very "comfortable in their discomfort!"

One day Chuang-tzu and a friend were walking along a riverbank. "How delightfully the fishes are enjoying themselves in the water!" Chuang-tzu exclaimed. "You are not a fish," his friend said, "How do you know whether or not the fishes are enjoying themselves?" "You are not me," Chuang-tzu said. "How do you know that I do not know that the fishes are enjoying themselves?" (Taoist Mondo)

CHAPTER TWO

Energy Packets

"Those who do not have power over the story that dominates their lives, the power to retell it, rethink it, deconstruct it, joke about it, and change it as times change – truly are powerless, because they cannot think new thoughts". (Salman Rushdie)

For those who have suffered multi abuses or traumatic occurrences, healing has been metaphorically likened to "peeling the various layers of onion skin" - processing the material and feelings layer by layer until such time as there is a sense of resolution, peace or dissolution. I have often used the metaphor of our soul being like that of an empty real estate lot upon which is built a foundation (beliefs), the design of which was dependent upon the actions and words of significant people in our early years. With very minimal input into this original design, our reactions to the world around us developed and a structure was built, based upon our original responses/reactions to different situations. For those who had "frozen" trauma images and feelings, the structure would appear like a skyscraper with no real variations in the design from the original.

Many similar situations in the present time will elicit the same type of reaction as a person experienced at the time of the original trauma. This suggests that it would be more efficient, and therefore hopefully less painful and time-consuming to work through the earliest known traumas that continue to recreate that unwanted reaction. This is in order to *implode* the other layers of the building that contain the same emotions, i.e. shame, guilt and, fear etc. If the layers are then worked through, it will also break apart the original foundation, through the reframing that would take place, i.e. recognizing that one was helpless, dependent and a victim. This would leave the original lot (soul) ready and waiting for a new foundation and building (fresh experiences and responses rather than reactions). This is as a result of finally having a true sense of choice, independence and, in this state, the willingness to be healthily vulnerable, to forgive, to love unconditionally, to befriend the self, and to be connected and comfortable with one's own spirituality (Higher Power). Most people who have been in an auto accident in which, for a split second beforehand, they 'knew' what was about to happen, but not the outcome, can relate to the following common fear-based reactions. The body goes taut, one stops breathing momentarily and we instantly "freeze" the image (still picture) of the moment that we felt that death or pain could be imminent. The treatment goal is therefore to "unfreeze" the image (picture), in order to allow the movie to "run on", so that all levels of one's consciousness and awareness truly know that one has survived, continued to grow up, and did not die. This allows for both a sense of inner peace and the dispelling of any self-sabotaging that may have otherwise surfaced. Core Belief Engineering is designed to reframe any harmful beliefs that appear stuck or frozen. To unfreeze such beliefs or cellular memory can change or shift the way we view or act in the present moment, or in the future.

Frozen development is the frozen vibration of the original trauma. This means that if it is not attended to and worked through, then similar vibrations in the present will create the same fear-based response. "In the extreme state of shock or terror, there is total immobility of the muscles, spinal cord, and the lungs, a defocusing of the eyes, and a partial congealing of the fluids and the arterial blood supply." (Keleman p. 66)

Energy healers may refer to "frozen psychic time conglomerates" as being when, from conception onwards, we had to stop the flow of energy around a particularly painful event, we froze that event in both energy and in time, which creates a frozen energy-consciousness. Any part of our psyche associated with that event also froze as we separated or dissociated, or otherwise stopped the pain. It is that part of the psyche that needs "thawing out", as it does not mature along with our physiology. It will not mature until conscious thought and energy get to the block and allow the processing to take place and allow for true maturation. The need is to turn any still/frozen fear, or anxiety images, into moving pictures, and thereby merge the levels of consciousness and allow for the natural flow of the body's energies again.

When studying and researching how and where memories were retained and recalled, Wilder Penfield, a Canadian neurosurgeon, stated, "It was evident at once that these (memories) were not dreams. They were electrical activations of the sequential record of consciousness, a record that had been laid down during the patient's earlier experience. The patient 're-lived' all that he had been aware of in that earlier period of time as in a moving-picture flashback." (Talbot p. 12)

It was Karl Pribram who determined that the brain, through its holographic nature, had the amazing ability to store a staggering amount of information, and that the frozen imagery of trauma can be accounted for by the blocking of the necessary interference, and resolved when the interference patterns are unblocked and returned to a flow state.

A person may continue to draw fear-based situations into their life in the form of re-enactment, and it follows that these reenactments will stop once there has been a resolution to the original trauma.

Theodore Millon described obsessions and compulsions as being similar to other neurotic symptoms in that they "reflect the operation of intrapsychic mechanisms."

Each neurotic disorder protects the individual from recognizing the true source of his anxieties, yet allows the anxiety a measure of release without damaging his self-image or provoking social rebuke. In phobias, the inner tension is symbolized and attached to an external object; in conversions, it is displaced and expressed through some body part; in dissociative symptoms, there is a blocking or splitting off of the anxiety source; in obsessions and compulsions, tension is controlled, symbolized and periodically discharged through a series of repetitive acts or thoughts. (p. 405)

The autonomic and central nervous systems govern the messages and automatic reactionary functions of the body. Therefore our heart rate, blood pressure, circulation, respiration, posture, and digestion can all be negatively impacted and lead to obvious physical tensions such as headaches.

Fritz Perls stated that, "Fear is the excitement without the breath." It has been established that for some there is a direct link between having panic attacks and alcoholism, and that hyperventilation and fear of dying can be a direct trigger for the need to "mood alter". (*Alcoholism Treatment Quarterly*. 1993. Vol.10. pps. 1-2)

As already stated, stress can also be said to come from three main sources; fear, pain, and fear of more pain, which in turn can produce "anticipatory anxiety". Proponents of the Three In One Concepts believe that *perceptions* of fear, pain and fear of more pain produce a Negative Emotional Charge (NEC). (Stokes/Whiteside p. 59) This is very relevant to the issue of reversals and corrections of same.

Some data involving phobics with symptoms that range from simple anxiety to full-blown phobias would suggest that the subconscious has become saturated by past traumatic events, which are unresolved, and therefore lead to the over-saturation (or total depletion) of chemicals and hormones that are designed to regulate us. The key lies in the ability of an anxious person to realize the truth that, "It's over, let it go, let it rest in peace. I can't change it, the past is over, my control is in the present, not the past nor the future!" (Sahley, 1994 p. 9) TFT and other AIP's allow this re-framing to be facilitated at the core subconscious level and does not require behavioral modification or constant affirmations - as these appear to be automatically and positively impacted.

It is known that a certain level of stress is necessary to

maintain optimal health. Hans Selye (a pioneer of research on stress and its origins and effects) referred to this optimal level as "Eustress" or "positive excitement". If this optimal level is exceeded and any form of system dysfunction follows, then that is referred to as "distress". (Gerber p. 440)

There is an obvious fear or phobic response as a result of something that has occurred in a traumatic fashion, or has a distinct possibility of happening, but, as has been stated, the body cannot tell the difference between what is real and what is imagined. This fits the acronym of FEAR (**F**alse **E**vidence **A**ppearing **R**eal). However, often a phobia begins following a trauma that has not been resolved, and the inner disturbance of energy can often manifest in some totally unrelated phobia. Phobias are certainly forms of distress and there are many of them. For a full list of common and unusual phobias, I would recommend reading Dr. James Durlacher's book *Freedom from Fear Forever*. (pps. 213-219)

Agoraphobia is a fairly common fear-based anxiety disorder and a handout entitled *Agoraphobia – the Grip of Fear* detailed the physiological response to stress and how it can lead to a particular phobia.

A person who finds himself in a dangerous or threatening situation responds with a "fight or flight" reaction. The mechanism is located in an area of the brain called the hypothalamus. When a person is threatened, the brain transmits a biochemical message and this causes the adrenal gland to produce adrenalin, which in turn sets off a general "call to arms" throughout the body. What happens in the body? The muscles tense, the pupils dilate, the heart beats faster, the blood pressure goes up, breathing increases, the stored sugar and fats flow into the blood stream, digestion ceases and all senses are heightened whether to real or imaginary demands. This state is temporary as the body cannot maintain it as a lasting condition. These biochemical responses to stress develop ulcers, headaches, skin disorders, insomnia etc. The panic disordered person's response to stress is a feeling of terror (panic) and subsequently the development of anticipatory anxiety, panic thinking and avoidance behavior that becomes agoraphobia.

(Se-Cure - J.C. Quinn workshop on phobias 20th April '94)

Fear can also provide "secondary gains", inasmuch as allowing us to avoid fulfilling our true individual potential. Abraham Maslow noted that the fear of our own higher potentialities is quite common. "We enjoy and even thrill to the godlike possibilities we see in ourselves in peak moments. And yet we simultaneously shiver with weakness, awe, and fear before these same possibilities. Fear of knowing is very deeply a fear of doing." (Ferguson p. 91)

Having knowledge carries with it responsibility, and once something has been made conscious to us we have choice – and if we do nothing to change things, then that in itself needs to be recognized as a choice. At least the gift of healing brings one back to a place where true choice is again (or for the first time) available. If one decides to do nothing differently, it is at least a decision made from a state of healthy reasoning ability, and not from one of psychological imprisonment, torment, or ignorance.

In a sense there is a need for reframing of the mind and/or re-patterning of the body to return it to a state of full integrity. This means in effect going back to the original action in order to heal it. This is a form of abreaction, but does not have to be in a totally literal sense, as one is more often than not able to "tune-in" to the experience and not be subject to what is called "exposure or confrontation" therapy. Good memories produce endorphins, whereas bad memories have a toxic impact. Memory is stored as vibration, strong emotions cannot get evoked if the body is in a total state of relaxation, therefore if one is able to remove muscle tension, then memory stored in that area of the body can be safely released.

In his research, Dr. Stanislav Grof noted that memories of emotional and physical experiences are stored in the psyche not as isolated bits and pieces but in the form of complex constellations, which he termed "COEX systems" (systems of condensed experience). He believes that each of these COEX systems consists of emotionally charged memories from different periods of our lives and that the common denominator that brings them together is that they share the same emotional quality or physical sensation. The COEX may have different layers, permeated by central themes, sensations and emotional qualities, and these layers can often be identified by the different periods in a person's life. Each COEX has a theme such as major events of humiliation, embarrassment, degradation, or shame. Another could be of all incidents that appeared to involve being abandoned. Any life-threatening incidents could lead to a frozen COEX state, which again can help us understand the energy packets that can be dissipated by energy healing. COEX packets are also made up of very pleasant memories. Therefore these packets influence the way we perceive the world, others and ourselves - they shape perceptions and reactions that echo the stored COEX systems, and can continually re-create negative or harmful experiences. (Grof p. 24) It is said that we will continue to re-enact until we have found resolution, therefore understanding the origins and the usefulness of our personal COEX systems can go a long way to getting back to a state of healthy homeostasis.

The energy packets then are the energy of the stuffed, repressed and unexpressed emotions – they lead to a desire to mood alter, to escape the pain and overwhelm – which leads to unhealthy relationships with people, processes and substances.

It has become a matter of Repression vs. Expression and repression, isolation and trauma is often at the centre of the creation of addictions, depression, anxiety and ultimate self-sabotage.

The goal becomes to move from being an Adversary to being an Advocate – to live 24/7 with a 'best friend' for company, bearing in mind that you are the only person you will never leave or lose.

YOU are also the world's leading authority on yourself and therefore are able to use, what I refer to as, the 'independent, expert, observer self'- that which knows all about you and has access to all of your wisdom, knowledge and life experience and can you use to direct your life in the direction of healthy thinking and action. If you were to live according to your wisdom and not slavishly to old stuck patterns of belief and behavior – then life would be one of being able to respond rather than react to any given situation.

It could be like having an internal committee of those you most admire, e.g. Nelson Mandela, Mahatma Gandhi, Mother

Teresa (or whomever you most admire) – sort of an internal round table – whose role it is to observe, support and guide you. This is actually a very good tool to support you in maintaining your personal set of values and goals in your decision-making.

With this particular internal committee, it is rather like asking "What would love do in this situation?"

CHAPTER THREE

The Template Trauma List

"What step(s) would I take if I were brave?" (Jana Stanfield)

Following assessment and a determination of a client's goals and comfort level with the possible use of AIP techniques, I will often suggest that they begin "befriending" themselves by making what I call a "chronological template trauma list". I suggest they take a sheet of paper and write in a vertical line the numbers one (1) through to whatever age they presently are. Then to write down any trauma that they actually remember alongside the age at which they were when it occurred. This is about honoring yourself and what has happened either directly to you or what you were witness to, just as you would if it were for someone you loved unconditionally. Could be a situation or situations of trauma, overwhelm or absolute helplessness. Abusive family situation could be watching a parent physically harm the other or a sibling.

In order to save any possible embarrassment or harm if the list were to be read by another person, I suggest that they note the trauma in such a way that only they can understand what it truly means and that, unless they wish to, they never have to share it. An example would be if a person was attacked by a dog at age seven, beside the number seven they could just put the word "dog". In some respects this can have a similar purpose to a step four, as in the addictions 12-step work. It helps the person identify and validate their truth, rather than what they have been told or led to believe was or was not traumatic for them. Working with the earliest listed traumatic memories that the client states have not been resolved, or that still bring up a painful resonance, disturbance perturbation, trigger, turmoil, physical or emotional reaction, i.e. fear, phobia or anxiety, is hopefully the beginning of "breaking up the foundation" and imploding the building of self-harming, self-defeating, and often self-medicating behaviors and beliefs.

Many similar situations in the present time will elicit the same type of reaction as a person experienced at the time of the original trauma. This suggests that it would be more efficient, and therefore hopefully less painful and time-consuming to work through the earliest known traumas that continue to recreate that unwanted reaction. This is in order to *implode* the other layers of the building that contain the same emotions, i.e. shame, guilt and, fear etc. If the layers are then worked through, it will also break apart the original foundation, through the reframing that would take place, i.e. recognizing that one was helpless, dependent and a victim. This would leave the original lot (soul) ready and waiting for a new foundation and building (fresh experiences and responses rather than reactions). This is as a result of finally having a true sense of choice, independence and, in this state, the willingness to be healthily vulnerable, to forgive, to love unconditionally, to befriend the self, and to be connected and comfortable with one's own spirituality (Higher Power).

CHAPTER FOUR

The Difference between Shock & Trauma

"Everyone wants to live on the peak of a mountain, without knowing that the real happiness is in how it is scaled."
Gabriel Garcia Marquez

Shock has the ability to obstruct our access to some of the deepest aspects of the Self - resulting in difficulties with intimacy, self-esteem, connection to one's sense of purpose and meaning, and spirituality. Shock is stored in the body and reactivated by events in daily life until it is resolved. It is mediated by unconscious rather than conscious aspects of the personality.

Unlike trauma, it is activated not only by stimuli resembling the original trauma, but also by many apparently unrelated triggers. Where trauma maximizes and hones physiological functioning, shock minimizes and impairs physiological functioning. Trauma still allows intimacy, while shock blocks intimacy. Emerson's work in explicating the differences between shock and trauma has made it clear that, along with appropriate psychotherapy protocols for treating shock, the physiological shock response requires treatment or it keeps *the individual in a constant state of `red alert` that eventually leads to adrenal fatigue and finally, adrenal exhaustion.*

Traumatized individuals have had some sense of control and efficacy while their traumatization is in process - fight or flight are successful to some degree in defending against or ameliorating the effects of the traumatizing agents. In shock, neither fight nor flight is successful. Overwhelm is what separates shock from trauma.

(*Insights* Magazine - B.C. Ass. Of Clinical Counsellors - `Pre- and Peri-natal Shock: Considerations for Psychotherapy` by Claire Winstone, pps. 8-24)

Shock will have major impact on both the psychological and physiological levels, including hormonal production such as adrenals and thyroid. Being in the aforementioned state of "red alert", or hyper-vigilance, over an extended period of time can have a devastating effect on the adrenals and lead to a state which is now commonly referred to as chronic fatigue.

Dr. Emmerson has also broken down shock into classifications of commission (event) or omission (need). There can be the single incident events such as abortion attempt, an epidural, c-section, physical or sexual abuse, sudden loss etc. or multiple incidents of not having basic needs met, i.e. neglect, indifference, a lack of touch or comfort. Damage of this sort will often make it difficult for a person to take in love and compassion when it is healthily available to them. A distrusting belief system can govern a lifetime of unhealthy relationships and potentially self-sabotaging actions.

In order for full emotional recovery to happen it is important to be open to the understanding that the genesis of any form of self-sabotage or stinking thinking is multi-faceted – hence the current addictions model is a bio/psycho/social/spiritual one. This should be borne in mind as we move through these chapters - compassion, understanding, love and action can lead to total transformation.

> "Neurosis is the avoidance of legitimate suffering".
> (Carl Jung)

CHAPTER FIVE

Surviving versus Thriving

"Life is the flower for which love is the honey."

(Victor Hugo)

What are the qualities that separate those who have the ability to withstand the worst and yet are seemingly still able to thrive, from those who catastrophise and view themselves as hapless and helpless victims?

People who are good copers are often referred to as *stress-hardy.* Psychologist Suzanne Kobasa has identified three attitudes that sustain such individuals during demanding times. These attitudes are called the three C`s: challenge, commitment, and control. A stress-hardy person sees change and crisis as a challenge rather than a threat. Even when they cannot control the outer situation, they realize that they always have control over their response to the things that are happening. There is a wise saying that relates to this phenomenon: "Suffering is inevitable, but misery is optional." (*Anatomy of an Illness* – Norman Cousins p. 26)

Listed below are some of the 'Thriver' qualities, which have been excerpted from '*The Beethoven Factor: The New Positive Psychology of Hardiness, Healing, and Hope*' by Paul Pearsall, Hampton Roads Publishing 2003.

Thrivers are beings who can creatively construe situations that allow themselves to develop an increasingly more encompassing and adaptive explanatory style.
They tend to have very strong immune systems and even at the worst of times, they seem aware on some level of the rules by which it functions.

They have faith that no feeling will last forever. The "Have Faith, Calm Down, and Don't Despair" rule.

They sense that suffering is essential for a truly authentic life.

They seem to know or have learned to let their emotions flow naturally rather than to cling to them. They know that it's not being afraid, depressed, or anxious that destroys their lives; it's allowing themselves to get stuck in these emotional states. The "Let It Go" rule.

They encounter trauma and are able to make meaning out of what happened (e.g. Viktor Frankl – *Man's Search for Meaning*), they are not only immunized against the next adversity, they also become better able to recover more quickly from it.

They not only find more to enjoy about life, but are much happier with much less.

They lower the threshold for being thrilled and forgive themselves for their own shortcomings and the world for its seeming random harshness, i.e. "It's a lot easier to feel great when you don't go around expecting life to be fantastic."

They can live, when necessary, with lower aspirations but realistically raise their inspiration.

They are not blindly optimistic and are far from showing the often-irritating, feigned cheerfulness.

They thrive because they mentally remain engaged with their problem long enough to find meaning that helps to accommodate to whatever happens to them.

"Most people would rather stagnate in the security of the known than evolve in the creative uncertainty of the unknown." (Linda Kohanov)

"Some would much rather complacently survive in a rigid hierarchy than thrive in the ambiguities of freedom." (Kohanov)

They continue to be the creative composers of their own consciousness.

Some of the signs of creative composition and inner peace are:

- Tendency to think and act spontaneously rather than from fear based on past experiences.
- An unmistakable ability to enjoy each moment.
- Loss of interest in judging other people.
- Loss of interest in judging self.
- Loss of interest in interpreting the actions of others.

- Loss of interest in conflict.

- Loss of ability to worry (a very serious symptom)

- Frequent, overwhelming episodes of appreciation.

- Contented feelings of connectedness with nature and others.

- Frequent attacks of smiling through the eyes from the heart.

- Increased tendency to let things happen rather than make them happen.

- Increased susceptibility to Love extended by others, as well as the uncontrollable urge to extend it.

(*Olympia Fellowship of Reconciliation Newsletter.* Issue. 63, 1986)

On the issue of being one's authentic self vs. the desire for attachment, regardless of the cost, Dr. Gabor Mate has stated that, most people, when faced with the choice of either attachment or authenticity in their relationships, will go for attachment first, seeking recognition and validation from others instead of being able to give it to themselves. In the majority of situations, most of us will decide that it's far more important for others to like us than for us to do whatever it takes to like ourselves. In other words for some, respect and acceptance from others trumps self-respect and self-acceptance pretty much all the time. (Candace Plattor-*Insights mag.* Aug 2012 – p. 28)

Bear in mind that a big part of the goal is to return to our authentic self or Spirit, as we were, in effect, Dis-spirited by trauma. It is interesting to note that the Latin word 'Spiritus' means alcohol, which therefore moves one into a state of 'artificial grace', whereby one becomes separated from Self. The benefits of healing trauma and shock and therefore thriving include moving from a Dissociated Self to Re-Connection, by Re-membering (bringing all parts of the self together) and releasing.

One metaphor for releasing would be like "popping a balloon" vs. "releasing the air" (i.e. the Energy Packets) Popping a balloon would be the goal for one incident of shock/trauma and releasing the air at a pace that was safe and healthy would be the goal for multiple incidents of shock/trauma.

Also bearing in mind that a person often seeks mood altering substances or processes in order to cover up anxiety and that it can be argued that every behavior has a positive intent (such as a desire not to feel anxiety - doesn't always by any means justify it though) – therefore the question of "Why do I continue to do this?" becomes one of "What good things do I (or others) get from this."

If you wish to look deeper into the issue of the nature of addictions, I would suggest my own book 'Rapid Recovery: Accelerated Information Processing & Healing' regarding energy medicine and the various tools and techniques and tune-ins and tune-ups that can be helpful and I have made some other reading recommendations as well as a bibliography and reference section at the end of this book.

"I'd rather be seen for who I am and be alone, than to be accepted for someone I am not and be lonely". (Brock Tully)

"He who cannot change the very fabric of his thought will never be able to change reality." Anwar Sadat.

"All stress is internally generated by one's attitudes." Dr. David Hawkins.

"The only thing I could change was my attitude and by changing that, everything changed." Anthony de Mello.

"The greatest discovery of any generation is that human beings can alter their lives by altering their attitudes of mind." Albert Schweitzer.

"Your life is determined not so much by what life brings to you as by the attitude you bring to life." Kahlil Gibran

"The longer I live, the more I realise the impact of attitude on life. Attitude, to me, is more important than facts. It is more important than the past, than education, than money, than circumstances, than failures, than successes, than what other people think or say or do. It is more important than appearance, giftedness or skill. It will make or break a company… a church… a home. The remarkable thing is we have a choice every day regarding the attitude we will embrace for the day. We cannot change our past…we cannot change the fact that people will act in a certain way. We cannot change the inevitable. The only thing we can do is play on the one string we have, and that is our attitude… I am convinced that life is 10% what happens to me and 90% how I react to it. And so it is with you… we are in charge of our Attitudes." Charles Swindoll

CHAPTER SIX

The Importance of Water

"A happy life consists not in the absence but in the mastery of hardships." (Helen Keller)

*Please make sure that you (Clinician and client) are well-hydrated at the beginning of a session for the purpose of "cleaning/clearing" and it is recommended that you have some on hand at the closure of a session too.

Water is an excellent conductor of electrical energy/current and when we are dehydrated there is interference with our body's energy flow. The body is made up of 70% water. A molecule of water is broken up into a positively charged hydrogen ion consisting of two hydrogen atoms, and a negatively charged oxygen ion consisting of one oxygen atom (Korzybski p. 686)

Magnetic resonance imaging is a system which utilizes the now familiar CT computer programs to produce pictures of the human body based on their reaction to high intensity magnetic fields. Of interest is the fact that current MRI images are based on the distribution and structured qualities of water within the tissues of the human body.

In their revised teachers' edition of *Brain Gym* (1994), Dr. Paul Dennison and Gail Dennison have written about the importance of water and its role in brain activation, academic skills, and its behavioural and postural correlates. (p. 24) Part of the Brain Gym course is in Edu-K(inesthetics), and exercises include PACE, which stands for **P**ositive, **A**ctive, **C**lear, and **E**nergetic.

To start a client off, the practitioner utilizes AK (Applied Kinesiology) testing following each of these four Brain Gym activities:

Positive - Doing Cook's Hook-Ups, which diffuse emotional or environmental stress.

The adrenal zip-up/down/up testing can also be done for the same purpose.

Active - Using cross-crawl, which activates the left and right cerebral hemispheres.

Clear - Rubbing the K-27`s (called brain buttons in Brain Gym), which stimulates neurotransmitter production at the synapses in the brain.

Energetic - Drinking sufficient water, which serves as the medium that conducts electricity within the body. (*Brain Gym 1 and 2*. Course Outline. pps. 4-6)

These exercises are in fact done in the reverse order, beginning with testing for hydration by the practitioner using AK while holding some of the client's head hair between the thumb and index finger. If the resistance is low, then the client should drink water and be re-tested until the resistance becomes strong and they are then sufficiently hydrated.

It is now generally believed it is the water in our bodies that regulates all functions of the body, including the activity of all the solutes that are dissolved in it. Your bones are a quarter water. The muscles that drive your performance are three-quarters water. If you dehydrate a muscle by only three per cent you cause about a 10 per cent loss of contractile strength and eight per cent loss of speed. ...When you become dehydrated a cascade of chemical events take place. Your body naturally begins to increase production of histamine. Histamine is present in all body tissues and produced by the mast cells found in connective tissue. Not only is histamine a mediator in inflammation, but it acts as a neurotransmitter, directing and operating the subordinate systems that promote water distribution to various tissues and organs. These subordinate systems involve the action of the hormones vasopresin and reninangiotensin, as well as prostaglandins and kinins. When levels become excessively active the mucus membranes of the lungs, for example, can become irritated and in time the muscles and tissues that make up the breathing mechanism can go into spasm, resulting in severe breathing problems and at worse asthma. This in addition to long term damage to the immune system, is bad news indeed for the athlete. (Christina Robilliard. *Athletics Weekly*. Sept 15th 1999 p. 22)

Lack of water is considered to be the number one trigger for daytime fatigue - even mild dehydration will slow one's metabolism down by as much as three per cent and some figures suggest that 75% of the population would be considered clinically dehydrated!

At a First Nations workshop with Lee Brown, an addictions counsellor, he made a presentation on the interpretation of dreams. It was interesting to hear that the most common belief about dreams that involve water is that the water will often represent emotions. Flowing water or drifting through water can mean that emotions are naturally being processed or brought to consciousness for recognition and processing, whereas frozen water or crystallized light will often mean that the person is in a state of emotional freeze, or is "numbed out". There are many books and articles on dream interpretation, but maybe the main thing we can look for are obvious signals regarding inner distress, and dreams that are recurring and have a `theme` to them, though it will most often show as a metaphor. If it is indeed our subconscious trying to give us remembrances of our unfinished business, and we choose to ignore it, then we should not be too surprised if we are later confronted with some physical issue that we can no longer ignore.

As demonstrated by the prototypical homeopathic remedies, vibrational characteristics are usually imprinted upon the universal storage medium of nature: water. The subtle energetic patterns stored within the vibrational essence may be used to affect human beings at a variety of interactive levels. (Gerber p. 242)

Note - For a full understanding of the impact of our thoughts, intentionality, images and prayers on water, I recommend reading '*Messages from Water*'. Author Masaru Emoto has done some brilliant research and provides stunning photographic images of crystallized water from worldwide sources and the amazing patterns/designs that are formed. Emoto provides clear and dramatic proof that water is truly a mirror reflecting our mind (thought forms).

1. 75% of Americans are chronically dehydrated. Likely applies to half the world's population.

2. In 37% of Americans, the thirst mechanism is so weak that it is mistaken for hunger.

3. Even MILD dehydration will slow down one's metabolism as much as 3%.

4. One glass of water will shut down midnight hunger pangs for almost 100% of the dieters studied in a University of Washington study.

5. Lack of water is the number one trigger of daytime fatigue.

6. Preliminary research indicates that 8-10 glasses of water a day could significantly ease back and joint pain for up to 80% of sufferers.

7. A mere 2% drop in body water can trigger fuzzy short-term memory, cause trouble with basic math and cause difficulty focusing on the computer screen or on a printed page.

8. Drinking 5 glasses of water daily decreases the risk of colon cancer by 45%, plus it can slash the risk of breast cancer by 79% and one is 50% less likely to develop bladder cancer.   Are you drinking the amount of water you should drink every day?

CHAPTER SEVEN

Neurological Disorganisation (Reversals) & Correction

"A willingness to be transformed is an essential characteristic of the participatory scientist" (Willis Harman - Talbot p. 290)

N.B. - If you are a therapist or practitioner then I heartily recommend that you always do the **Collarbone Breathing** exercise with your client to demonstrate how to correct, enhance or maintain your own positive energy and neurological status. Benefits are well-being, coordination, clarity of thinking, balance, strength, ability to make wise decisions when under mental and physical duress or stress.

The **N**eurological **D**isorganization correction procedure, which Dr. Roger Callahan referred to as **Collarbone Breathing**, is as follows:

Place the right index finger and middle finger on the soft tissue point just below the left side collarbone (K-27). With the left hand index and middle finger of the left hand, tap the gamut spot (on the back of the hand, between the baby finger and index finger) while breathing in fully and deeply, hold the breath, let out half the breath, then the other half, then breathe in a half breath. Breathe normally for a few moments and then do the same with the other hand, i.e. left fingers now over to the right K-27 point and, with the index and middle finger of the right hand, tap the gamut spot and do the same tapping and breathing sequence. That connects the right brain to the left side, and vice versa. Then it needs to be done homolaterally, i.e. the right hand fingers on the right K-27 point, the same tapping and breathing sequence, and then the same with the left hand fingers on the left K-27 point.

As a bonus for all the times a therapist may demonstrate this exercise, they will probably find subtle or significant improvements in their own sense of well-being, overall coordination, and clarity of thinking.

Such techniques have been noted as effective for schizophrenics (Walther/Wakefield/Flint), as well as for dyslexia and other learning difficulties, and for improvement of coordination and physical gait.

For athletes, the benefits include the sense of well-being, balance, coordination, strength and ability to make wise decisions when under any form of mental or physical duress/stress.

Dr. Callahan describes Psychological Reversal (PR) as being a state or condition which blocks natural healing and prevents otherwise effective treatments from working. Dr. John Diamond referred to it as the *"Reversal of the Body Morality"*. A person may be fine in most domains of his/her life and be in a state of PR in just one area or a selected few. This PR state is usually accompanied by negative attitudes and self-sabotaging behavior. It can be as simple as saying East when you mean West or more seriously, as in dyslexia, whereby the sufferer may write upside down or backwards. A massive PR is a reversal in most areas of life, and a mini reversal is a block, which kicks in during treatment and prevents the treatment from being complete. A recurring PR is a reversal, which returns as soon as it is corrected.

One of the sometimes frustrating and elusive goals that we have as individuals can be the search for, and attainment of, our full potential. That can prove to be a never-ending journey, and maybe at some level it is meant to be, so that we can continue to learn and grow. However, when it is painfully obvious that a person has all the right attributes but never quite "makes it", one needs to look beyond the obvious and look at what other factors may be involved.

Many of the clients I see can fully relate to the fact that at times they are their "own worst enemy", i.e. they know one thing, but do another. This is a state of self-sabotage and is, in effect, THE factor that needs to be recognized and treated/shifted in order for the path to potential and possibilities to be cleared. In fact addiction has been called a "reversal of intent", i.e. loss of control, whereas dependency can be viewed as being when one has made a choice to continue usage, despite the known consequences. (*Rational Recovery*. Jack Trimpey, p. 57) Although with my clients we are mainly talking sabotage as it relates to addictions, I have worked with a number of athletes who have identified that the same issue has resulted in a lack of transference from their training intensity and times to actual performance and race results.

There are many examples on a world class level whereby an athlete performs well at a National, Provincial, or State level, but then moves up to a major Games and consistently seems to "flunk" the opportunity to excel or to even perform to the level of expectation. Even at the local club level, many of us may speak about someone who appears gifted/talented but never quite pulls off the performances that their training would suggest they could. It may be that they pull out an occasional great race but lack consistency, or that they drop out of races for the slightest of reasons. In my role as a race announcer I have, on occasion, been able to clearly see when someone is going through the motions but has internally given up, yet on paper may have been the undisputed favorite.

This self-sabotage is not about a lack of ability or effort, and nor is it necessarily about a lack of desire. One has to recognize the role of the mind/body connection and how "What the mind dwells on, the body reveals." Again it should be remembered that this self-sabotage, which from this point on I shall refer to as a state of "reversal", can impact every aspect of our daily life – work, relationships, play, money, self-worth etc. Many of us have experienced the feeling or have clearly stated that we are having, or have had, "one of those days". We have usually meant that nothing appears to have gone in our favor, or that no matter what we do, nothing appears to be turning out "right". This is what is meant by the phrase "being in a state of reversal".

There are some simple ways to demonstrate how statements, thoughts, images, beliefs and substances can either be compatible to us or throw us into a state of reversal. As I have previously stated, I personally like to use AK (MRT or CRA) as the testing modality.

Whisenant describes PR as being "one of the most intriguing phenomena of AK" and states that PR is:

...a functional condition in which the left and right sides of the brain and subsequently the right and left sides of the body are communicating diametrically different messages. It results from an overstressing of the organism in any of a number of ways. It can be a nutritional deficit, an environmental toxin or other chemical stressor, a physical assault, a prolonged exposure to temperature extremes, or the shock of an emotional upset. This condition has been labeled Neurological Switching or Psychological Reversal. When a person is Switched, there will be one side of the body that has been overemphasized. It seems that all of us have a favored mode of dealing with stressors and that mode dictates which side of the body will become overstressed. The method of discerning which side of the body is overloaded involves first finding a strong indicator muscle when the person is relaxed and looking straight ahead. Then the person is instructed to shift the eyes to one side and the muscle is retested after which the eyes are shifted to the other side and the muscle is again retested. If there is a weakness when the eyes are looking to one side, that indicates the state of being Neurologically Switched. Because of the effects of certain

stated affirmations and goals this condition is also called
Psychological Reversal. (p. 15)

A state of reversal was often called "resistance". It is not a moral issue, except possibly when it is consciously known and has resulted in illegal or harmful behavior, and a person chooses not to do anything about it. However, it is sure nice to know that we have the ability to self-correct it, whenever we choose to, with no cost attached, no pills necessary, and no negative side effects.

The aspect of the body's energy system known as the conception vessel is meant to move upwards from the perineum to the bottom lip, while the governing vessel comes up the back, over the head and down to the upper lip, just under the nose. When the energy of the conception vessel is running downward instead of from the perineum to the bottom lip, then one's system is in a state of reversal.

As previously stated, the body cannot tell the difference between what is real and what is imagined. We know this as humans often have a physiological reaction to dreams/nightmares. We can therefore, wake up in the morning, not even remembering that we have had a dream, or one which contained something our system/subconscious perceived as "negative". Then throughout the rest of the day may have found that one is tripping over things, figuratively and literally, saying East when meaning West. Many may relate to it as being when you feel or state that you have been having "one of those days". This is when we tend to go against our own best interests, self-sabotaging, living in a state of paradox or ambivalence, i.e. "knowing one thing, but doing another."

Some people create mountains out of molehills (molehill mountain climbers) and thereby create a pattern of anticipated disasters, always expecting the worst case scenario plus! The psychologist Albert Ellis coined the term "awfulizing" for this phenomenon, and it has much to do with one's personal purview and expectation, making the need for healthy perceptual shift an essential, in order that our best potential or the highest good can manifest.

Some healthcare practitioners, usually chiropractors and psychotherapists, use the term "neuro-emotional complex" (NEC) to describe an emotional response to a significant life event that has gotten "locked" into one's sympathetic nervous system. This may later manifest as a spinal subluxation, and a specific imbalance in a muscle or acupuncture meridian, thereby resulting in some form of ill health.

These same practitioners, like chiropractor Mike Greenberg of Brentwood, California (who worked with Track & Field Olympic gold medalists Kevin Young and Quincy Watts), use Neuro Emotional Technique (NET) to address the emotional component of a problem through spinal adjustment, similar in some way to Torque Release Technique. A branch of NET is Neuro Emotional Anti-Sabotage Technique (NEAT), the purpose of which is to make certain that the client is congruent with whatever is desirable. AK can be used on simple statements such as, "I want to change the situation" and by analyzing that which is *not* okay, a subluxation adjustment can be made for correcting same. This would appear to be identical to the concept of "reversals" and "correcting reversals."

Practitioners of Somato Emotional Release refer to Energy Cysts (EC) as being the residual localized energy which has been introduced into a client's body by external physical trauma, emotional trauma, pathogenic microbes of any type, exposure to excessive radiation and toxic substances. If the body is incapable of releasing or dissipating this externally induced energy, it remains as an EC – a form of disorganized, negative energy. John Upledger (*CranioSacral Therapy*. Illinois, Eastland Press. 1983) states that body cells and tissues (muscle, bone, teeth, fascia or other connective tissues or viscera) have the ability to retain memories of experienced trauma, and that the memory's emotional energy also gets stored and may get stimulated by the placing of a therapist's hands on the area of the emotional trauma.

Kahlil Gibran said that,"Pain is the bitter pill of the inner physician that cracks the shell of our understanding." A seed can only grow into a flower when it has swelled and died. Likewise, our own ability to create newness in our lives comes from periods of crisis that force us to put (some of) our old behaviors and beliefs to rest. (Borysenko p. 83)

Anxiety, fear, painful memory, anticipation, stuck ego beliefs/protection, toxins, allergies, pollutants etc. can all create the effect of reversal. For some, it can have links with an original sense of not getting unconditional love or acceptance – therefore some level of self-rejection may occur and a belief that one doesn't deserve success/wealth etc. (Janov p. 71)

Imagine what would be happening to your energy system if your thoughts, when in any form of competition, (running for example), turned to self-doubts; "I don't know if I can do this." "I'm alongside John S. and he is much faster than me –

I shouldn't be here – I've gone off too fast – can't hold the pace – have never gone this far/fast before." "It's too hot/cold/far/hilly/rough/windy – I never race well in these conditions." "I hate a sprint finish – have never beaten anyone in a sprint before – what's the point – suffering sucks!" "I'm at 20 miles, this is where everyone tells me I'm going to 'Hit the Wall'.", and so on. It is worthwhile using AK to test your resistance when you make those statements aloud, without even being in a race situation! Check it out also on any negative statements you may have found yourself using regarding any situations that you may have encountered or are currently involved in.

For runners, I suggest that a clearer and more practical demonstration can be noted when timing oneself on say a hard 800m or one kilometer run, while constantly repeating in one's head the words, "I can do it." Then, after sufficient rest, run the same distance with the same level of intensity, but repeating the words, "I can't do it."

Then check to see the difference in time and how you feel after the two runs. Try it again a week later, but reverse the order of the statements. My guess is you will notice a difference in the times and the level of comfort both mentally and physically.

When physical attributes such as speed, stamina, strength, suppleness and skill are virtually equal, the advantage in a closely contested race lies with the athlete who has the better mental edge. The objective of psychological preparation is optimum arousal of the athlete's mental, physical and spiritual resources – along with a realistic assessment of his/her capabilities and training or racing goals. Self-oriented thoughts such as the fear of finishing last or not running up to expectations are negative, destructive and purposeless. Conversely, task oriented thoughts are constructive, positive and purposeful. They reduce anxiety, fear and stress levels. They enable the athlete to fulfill his/her potential and to do justice to training efforts. ('Mind over Matter'. Derek Parker. *Veteran Athletics* Magazine. Spring 1997, p. 23)

Peggy Claude-Pierre, who specializes in eating disorders, has coined the term Confirmed Negativity Condition (CNC). She wrote that, "An eating disorder victim must have CNC. Other possible negating manifestations of CNC may include depression, agoraphobia, panic attacks, obsessive-compulsive disorder, or somatic disorders (including any other way such victims may internalize their pain)." (p. 36) She also states that, "In order to correct the eating disorder symptom, the CNC *must be addressed and reversed.*" (ibid. p. 87)

In other words, "When you are in a hole, STOP DIGGING."

There is a very resistant form of reversal which William Whisenant termed "schizoid-reversal" as it is invariably present in schizophrenics. (p. 61) However, it could prove to be worthwhile having a combined medication and daily AIP routine or energy correction and prevention algorithm protocol.

The AIP's (Thought Field Therapy, Tapas Acupressure Technique and Emotional Freedom Techniques) that I utilize in my counseling, all work on the basis of giving attention to the problem (addressing it), correcting any reversal, and then releasing the blockage, disturbance, or perturbation in the body's energy system.

The origins of these reversals can create emotional and/or physical blockages, which thereby stunt possibilities and potential, and creates "neurological backfiring" and negative cellular memory, such as have been written about by such luminaries as Alice Miller (*For Your Own Good*).

I will not go into great detail here as to how to clear major traumas etc., but I wish to provide a simple, easy-to-follow protocol procedure for prevention and correction on a daily basis, so that your full self may always allow for biopsychosocialspiritual congruency and clarity of choices.

There are four reversal correction points that I would ask readers to consider and test out for themselves. These are ones that I use on a daily basis, first thing in the morning, and then again if anything has happened during the day that has caused some obvious energy disturbance, or if I realize that my reactions/responses are not coming from a healthy perspective.

The **first** one is to do what has been called the "**adrenal massage**", or in other words, stroking up the conception vessel. This is accomplished by placing the index finger on one side of the belly button and the middle finger on the other side, pressing the fingers into the skin and stroking them up to the neck. When you get to that point, take the hand a few inches away from the body and repeat about ten times. Do not bring the fingers or hand back down the conception vessel as that will send you into reversal. One can use AK to test this, but always finish by stroking upwards.

The **second** is usually for major (persistent) psychological reversal, but I use it on a daily basis.

The Neurolymphatic Reflex (NR) - (see also further explanation below by Dr. Lee Pulos)

Take two fingers and on your left side, press into the area around the heart (side of the compassionate heart chakra) and notice if you have a point on you, in that area, which feels more tender than anywhere else. If so, take the two fingers, keep them pressed into the center of that spot and then turn the fingers clockwise around that tender spot (kneeding). This acts as a way of dissipating the build-up of matter - getting it back into proper circulation.

This has an impact on the heart chakra, in which area sits the thymus, pericardium, lung and of course the heart. "When there is a blockage of pranic flow through the heart chakra because of problems in manifesting love towards self and others, there is a diminution of vital energy flow to the thymus gland." (Gerber p. 381) and "…thereby susceptibility to various bacterial and viral infections." (ibid. p. 383) It also helps strengthen your ability to give and receive love (from the self as well as from others). It is necessary to run the persistent reversal point in a clockwise direction, i.e. "When the chakras are functioning normally, each will be 'open', spinning clockwise to metabolize the particular energies needs from the universal field. A clockwise spin draws energy from the UEF (Universal Energy Field) into the chakra, very much like the right-hand rule in electromagnetism, which states that "a changing magnetic field around a wire will induce a current in that wire." (Brennan p. 71) The electrical wave produced by the beating heart has about fifty times the amplitude and about a thousand times the strength of the brain wave. As a result of this the heart tends to pull the brain and other organs into synchronization or "entrainment" with its rhythm, much like that of pendulum clocks whereby they will synchronize the ticking to that of the clock with the largest pendulum. (Eden p. 156)

Glen Rein of the Institute of HeartMath speculates that crystal-like structures in the heart serve as transducers for converting and integrating higher-dimensional energies into the electrical system of the human body, producing electrical frequency data reflected in the ECG. (*Brain/Mind Bulletin.* Jan '94 p. 8)

The heart's electromagnetic qualities act on matter in a similar fashion to a magnet with iron filings, and therefore matter that is not dissipated attracts and builds up in the heart area and causes clogging and pain i.e. such as what we might call a "broken' heart".

Some further validation of this point has come from Dr. Lee Pulos, who wrote that:

The PR can be corrected by rubbing the neurolymphatic reflex (NR), located bilaterally just above the pectoral muscle and immediately adjacent to the anterior deltoid muscles. This acts as an electrical reset button, reconnecting the relevant circuitry. The lymphatic system is made up of valves that allow lymph fluid to flow towards the heart. The primary function of this system is to remove debris or toxins from the interstitial spaces. Lymph flow is quite slow in order to break down the debris, which cannot be passed directly into the blood stream. Rubbing the neurolymphatic reflex helps the body to 'turn on' other reflex points or 'switches' downline to increase lymph drainage. In other words, it is not the flow of the lymph which brings about the change, but the stimulation of a specific electrical communication system which activates a series of impulses which allow the body to communicate more effectively with itself. Thus subconscious blockages and self-sabotage patterns are removed so that the treatment will be 'accepted' by the body. A useful metaphor for psychological reversals is to think of the subconscious fear as an overload that has come on-line. The effect is much like plugging too many electrical appliances into one outlet, which can blow a fuse. In terms of the body's energy, overload is a polarity imbalance (which relates to the body's left/right magnetic–electric fields and electron spin), which reverses muscle responses – yielding a 'no' for 'yes' and vice versa. Thus, the NRs act like circuit breakers that get turned off when the body/mind is overloaded (with fear, anxiety, energy toxins, etc.). (*Shared Visions* Magazine. May 1999, p. 37)

Self-sabotaging, or self-destructive thinking, and action, or inaction, which is often just procrastination, can lead to a very pessimistic outlook. It can therefore also be said that having such a switched circuit can lead to, or at least can be linked to, depression and create great reluctance to look at possibilities or opportunities for healthy change.

The procrastinator's creed might be something like, "I firmly believe that tomorrow holds the possibility for new technologies, astounding discoveries, and a reprieve from my obligations."

Procrastination is the ego trying to protect us, but it is doing so based on outdated information!

Gary Craig has equated this state to one in which the body's main battery has been turned or installed upside down and therefore the power in it cannot be accessed until it has been corrected or turned around. These emotional blockages create abnormal patterns in the heart chakra.

Scientist Itzhak Bentov researched a link between the heart and brain in meditation, which could cause lasting changes in the brain and bodily functioning. He discovered a system of tuned rhythmic oscillators were driven by circulatory pulses coming from the heart (Gerber p. 402)

Bipolar electromagnetic fields, such as the field of Earth itself, are *torus* (doughnut) shaped. Iron filings close by a standard magnet will assume a two-dimensional torus shape by arranging themselves along the magnet's lines of force. By placing hundreds of electrodes around the human heart, Arthur Winfree (*When Time Breaks Down*) of the University of Arizona discovered that the heart's electrical field takes the shape of a torus. Interestingly the torus also crops up repeatedly in graphic depictions of the strange attractors of chaos theory. (*Brain/Mind Bulletin*. January 1994, p. 8)

I have mentioned elsewhere that in a sense we need to have an "emotional enema", as well as possibly a physical one. Dr. Richard Gerber states that for good health we should have a constant and unimpeded energy flow at all levels of our energy system. He uses the analogy of plumbing, in which one must have adequate water input, no blockages or sewage in our pipes, and an opened release valve for water to optimally flow through the system. (p. 475)

The heart chakra is affected by one's ability to feel love towards the self as well as towards others. Those who are unable or unwilling to could be referred to as being "hard-hearted."

The heart chakra has an energy link to the thymus gland, and therefore the immune system, so our ability to be open to love and receive love can have a direct correlation to our immune system's integrity. (ibid. p. 433)

Researchers discovered that the blood of normal individuals has a subtle energetic quality associated with the clockwise rotation of polarity. It has been found that individuals living in regions associated with geopathic stress tended to have a counter-clockwise rotational polarity (in a state of reversal) in their blood. Interestingly, and not surprisingly, it has also been found that individuals with this abnormal polarity who are ill are usually resistant to any form of subtle energetic or vibrational medicine intervention, and secondly a majority of cancer patients possess this counter-clockwise blood polarity. As well as some of the reversal correction techniques mentioned herein, there are electroacupuncture and radionic systems, such as the Mora device, which can be used to reverse the blood polarity and make an individual more amenable to vibrational healing techniques. (ibid. p. 461)

Neurological Switching or Reversal can be temporarily induced for demonstration purposes by contacting the K-27's and massaging them in a counter-clockwise direction (Whisenant p. 18) This switch can then be easily tested by using AK. First test after a clockwise massage on the K-27's, in which case the resistance should test strong, then do a counter-clockwise massage and re-test, and you should notice a much weaker resistance.

The **third** reversal correction point I would recommend would be tapping the side of the hand (**karate chop point**) about ten times. This is the small intestine acupuncture/acupressure spot and is used by Dr. Callahan (TFT), Gary Craig (EFT) and Dr. Whisenant (PK).

If AK is done on someone who is focusing on a "negative" image, meaning something that the person doesn't like – a person, food, chore, place etc., and the arm goes weak or lacks resistance, tap the karate-chop point (S.I.), then re-test on the same image. It should then show a major improvement in the level of resistance. That is to say that the person's energy need not go into reversal when having that thought or any "anticipatory anxiety" about that issue.

The small intestine has been called the controller of the transformation of matter, which can "create changes of the physical substance."

The Small Intestine is in charge of separating the "pure" from the "impure". Not only food, but also thoughts and information, feelings and emotions, sights and sounds need to be sorted, so that which is valuable or "pure" can be used, and that which is useless or "impure" can be discarded. Imbalance of the S.I. meridian can correlate with assimilative problems, on the physical or psychological level. (Teeguarden 1987, pps. 106-7)

The small intestine meridian connects to under the cheekbones and ends next to the ear. Treating the small intestine has a beneficial effect on all mucus-related problems in the human body, i.e. watery discharge. In addition, regular treatment of the S.I. is effective against poor digestion, constipation and irregularities in the menstrual cycle. (Hadeler p. 20)

"Colloids, particularly in organisms, are extremely sensitive and complex structures with enormous possibilities as to degree of stability, reversibility, and allow a wide range of variation of behavior." (Korzybski p. 113) Was he referring to what we call meridians and reversals?

The **fourth** reversal correction point is directly under the nose, (sometimes called the "**Peak Performance**" point) which is the end of the governing vessel. This point should be tapped concurrently by the index and middle finger. This particular point appears to be very helpful for those who have memory blocks, such as when faced with an exam. Many people can be well prepared in terms of their studies, but suffer from 'mind-freeze' or 'going blank' once they have to produce the answers. For schoolchildren it can be used, along with the other correction points, while their attention/focus/mindfulness is on the subject that they seem to have the most difficulty with. A.K. should precede, and follow, the use of the correction points so that one is able to see the difference in the level of resistance once a correction has been made.

I have no proprietary interests in any of the tools/therapies/systems/techniques that I use and am only suggesting that if you feel that you wish to challenge any self-sabotaging/potential blocking thoughts or actions, it is only an investment of a few seconds a day for a month that might allow you to notice a difference in how you think about, respond to, or perceive the world and your Self. The reason for me suggesting at least a month is because studies have shown that it takes that amount of time of conscious effort to produce a new habitual response.

Again, there are many other possibilities for further exploration on specific issues, but for generalized positive energy I suggest that you start by keeping it simple and using the four reversal correction points first thing in the morning, and then as and when you feel you need to shift any negative energy.

The protocol in a nutshell;

1. The adrenal massage/zip-up.

2. Tender spot near heart (neurolymphatic reflex), clockwise rub.

3. Tap side of the hand – karate chop point.

4. Tap under the nose – the Peak Performance point.

What is meant by disorganization? It has been defined as
"…the act of disorganizing

1) to destroy the organic structure or regular or systematic arrangement of,
2) deprive of organization,
3) throw into disorder or confusion."

The body, when functioning normally, operates in a predictable, logical, organized manner. If some factor from the structural, chemical, or mental side of the triad of health creates an imbalance of function, signals are developed for the body to attempt to return itself to normal in the fastest, most efficient manner.

There is an optimum function for the organism. When it is not functioning at this level, it is disorganized. (Walther p. 131)

David Walther separates those backup systems that allow us to survive the disorganizations, into those which result from "predictable" and "unpredictable" disorganization, i.e. that which appears understandable, and that which seems random, haphazard and confused.

On a structural level some "predictable disorganization" might be that one physical aspect is not functioning properly, but that the origin is from a dysfunctional part of the system elsewhere. Certain individuals who have been exposed to extensive trauma, stress, environmental pollution or allergic reactions, may develop a heightened sensitivity to certain substances. While allergies affect the immune system, energy toxins interfere with and compromise the energy or meridian. Chemically, there are many possible negative influences on the body, such as environmental toxicity, medications, as well as foods and supplements that we may consume. Certain shampoos, detergents, perfumes, colognes, wheat, corn, cheese, alcohol and caffeine products can profoundly disrupt the energy system, so that few or no positive effects can be achieved by energy tapping. These offending substances can be identified by muscle testing (AK), and the toxic substance should be removed, or if that is not possible, the person should move to a different room or environment.

At the mental level, ongoing stress can occur as a result of hypoadrenalism, which affects so many things, including hormone and autonomic nervous system balance, as well as regulation of carbohydrates. The use of antidepressants and tranquilizers can often cause unpredictable disorganization, which will often show up when using AK.

AK practitioners will often refer to "switching" (another term for disorganization or being in a state of reversal). They will test for switching by evaluating the K-27 point, the governing and conception vessels, and for "ocular lock". For the latter, have the patient turn both eyes as far as possible in one direction, while testing a previously strong indicator muscle for weakening. If the body cannot maintain its neurologic integrity and the indicator muscle weakens, then this is what is known as "ocular lock". This should also be done with the eyes looking right, left, up, down and at angles. Stimulation of the K-27's should be able to temporarily correct this and allow for the present highest potential for healing.

Dr. Walther states that, "Our experience shows that evaluation of these factors will find nearly all conditions of switching in the body. The evaluation for switching should continue throughout the course of a patient's treatment, on every visit. The most common error leading to poor results with a patient is failure to eliminate switching and general neurologic disorganization. Whenever switching continues to return, the prognosis for regaining the highest possible plateau of health is poor." (p. 134)

One of the easiest ways to recognize signs of disorganization is in the reversal of actions or thoughts, like when someone does the opposite of what is being requested or says the opposite of what they mean. It really is the direct opposite, i.e. saying East when meaning West, but not saying North when meaning West. You will sometimes notice it when getting a client to do ND correction, asking them to use the right hand and they use the left instead, or state that they can't tell their right from their left, or always get confused over which is which.

Even stuttering, or its history is often caused by switching. The stuttering may be overcome but the neurologic disorganization that was the original cause may remain and cause other health problems.

CHAPTER EIGHT

Inner Dialogue

"Always be a first-rate version of yourself, instead of a second-rate version of somebody else." Judy Garland

Why do I recommend that one does some 'inner dialogue' prior to doing some processing of any shock/trauma? I believe it is practical and wise to 'ground' in the here and now.

This 'grounding' provides for present-day self-awareness and mindfulness and can lead to decisions and action steps from a place of courage, now knowing the outcome of the origins, rather than remaining in the fear/frozen state of an unknown outcome at its genesis.

As a result of any 'anticipatory anxiety'- the system is already reacting to how it was historically by the acknowledgement of the ongoing disturbances brought on by the internal 'energy packets' and, to this end, 'grounding' in the present reminds all 'parts' of the self of one's current status - including safety.

If you are a therapist then you would request that the client "relax as much as is possible under the circumstances" – if you are doing the work on and for yourself then just make these statements internally, including the command to relax as much as possible under the circumstances and the rest that follow.

As the therapist state that "Inside, to yourself, using whatever words you are comfortable with, let every 'part' of you know that, regardless of whatever has happened to you or around you, in the past, you have survived."

"Let every part of you know that you have grown up."

"That it is the year ------."

"That you have a right to breathe fully and deeply at all times"

Clearly state "Let every 'part' of you know that, regardless as to what has happened to you or around you in the past, you did not die."

Then, at a steady pace, when it seems appropriate, say, "…and now, please take a moment inside and, if you sense that some of this information is not believed by any part of you, then ask every part of you to become fully aware of the adult male/female body in which you presently reside."

"Remind every part of you about who you are today, where you are today and what you know today - that you could never have known at the time this occurred."

One is now readied for the processing action steps that follow.

CHAPTER NINE

Template Memories

"Now is the time to act. Why? Because it is too late to do it sooner!" (Swami Beyondananda)

September 11th 2001

A day that the world will never forget.

Seeing the terrifying images repeated so many times - many not feeling able to turn away from their TV screens. The repetitive showing of the planes crashing into the buildings, and the mind`s ability to have empathy and horror at the thought of what it must have been like to be in the planes or the buildings. To hear the telephone calls from those who were being hostages to the terrorists' suicidal plans, and to hear the very personal stories from the victims' family members. Critical Incident Stress Debriefing teams were immediately called into action especially for the police, fire, and emergency personnel.

Following this tragedy, my own experience demonstrated the power of the simplest technique. All my clients who have requested working on the trauma of September 11th have stated that the issue for them has been the inability to clear or dissipate the image of the planes crashing into the World

Trade Center buildings. Just like the newspaper and magazine front covers, the image was for each client a particular frozen frame image.

All the clients were reporting an inability to sleep, increasing anxiety and loss of function in work, play or relationships. One had totally returned to major self-destructive behaviors, though many addiction experts might suggest this just provided the perfect reason for relapse. However, this was someone who had clearly and cleanly been on a healing path for a good period of time. The images had become what I refer to as `template` memories, which prevent the ability to tune-in to pleasant thoughts. This type of `template` memory can occur when someone has witnessed a loved one die in a painful way, such as wasting from cancer, and that memory dominates all others and doesn`t allow for the surfacing of the many pleasant pre-wasting images.

What was the simple technique?

I just asked each of them to close their eyes and focus on that frozen image, and then to take two fingers of both hands and place them either side of the bridge of the nose and the beginning of the eyebrows (part of TFT trauma routine) and tap. After a few seconds they all reported that the images had "unfrozen" and was clearing, dissipating or just moving on.

Each also noted a dramatic drop in the level of anxiety they`d felt when they first "tuned-in", and have since reported a return to a healthier homeostasis, but with a great deal of care, concern, and compassion about the September 11th terrorist attacks.

As for the client who relapsed, he reports that his life is totally back on track again.

If this simple tapping technique does not seem effective in terms of clearing or dissipating the frozen image, then I will usually do what I call the `Inner Child/Adult Self-Reclamation` exercise, which is detailed later in this book.

The strongest or most dominant thought wins! We need to therefore stop giving the negative ones any life, power or control.

I`ve had some clients who have spent a great deal of time and energy trying to right some of the world`s wrongs, or trying to achieve some sense of fairness or justice in a particular arena, only to be consistently upset or deflated by the ongoing hurts and pain they feel as little or no progress appears to be made. I believe it is necessary for us all to realize that as humans we will never correct all the injustice or unfairness in the world. This is not to suggest that we should not do whatever we can to rectify things. But we need to do so with conscious understanding that, if it is our calling, then it`s important to do what we feel we can, but to not have our spirit so totally invested in the outcome that we become dis-spirited, exhausted, and overwhelmed.

Although activity absorbs anxiety, it is ACTION that challenges beliefs.

"Exercise is the chain that links us to the Chariot of wellbeing. Wellbeing means happiness, but happiness is also an attitude, and the best attitude is one of gratitude."

(Gerald Puls, Colorado. 75+ age group Ironman competitor)

CHAPTER TEN

TAT Pose & the Three-Spot Tapping Points

(The simplest cleaning and clearing method)

"Let your hopes, not your hurts, shape your future."
(Robert Schuller)

If a person has had multiple traumas, then start with the earliest known issue that you or our client has an image or memory of. I recommend this be done in chronological order so that the metaphorical foundation of the trauma high-rise building blocks can begin to crumble the rest of the building. Break the foundation away and then some of the floors will disintegrate and dissolve, as they will often contain many of the similar emotional elements of later trauma occasions and this foundation breaking allows implosion and dissolution to begin.

At this point, not knowing whether it is shock (frozen) or trauma (moving) that one is dealing with, we begin with the simplest cleaning and clearing method.

The method – have the client go into the TAT pose - Jane Wakefield's fingertips shell-like around the ears (see author's photo below), i.e.- place the fingertips gently on the head in a shell-like fashion around the ears, with the thumb at the bottom, and the pinky finger near the temple, until integration has occurred.

Ask the client (demonstrate if therapist or do so for yourself if you are working on a personal issue) to close their eyes and put their attention on the memory or image and to breathe fully and deeply from the diaphragm. Then ask if it is stuck or frozen, like a still photograph - or is it moving, like a movie picture?

If it is moving, then ask them to just watch/observe until it comes to some sense of completion/closure or if it 'freezes' at any point, to let you know.

If it is or does become stuck and frozen – that is when to use the Three-Spot tapping points. **Please see diagram below for the tapping spots.**

1. Take index and middle fingers of both hands and place them on the Bridge of the nose and beginning of the eyebrows – (third eye spot, pineal gland – crystalline substance). Tap there for about ten seconds as you continue to observe the memory – You can tap fairly solidly and rapidly without hurting yourself.
2. Tap the sides of the eyes for about ten seconds while observing the memory– this point is for anger/rage.
3. Tap under the eyes for about ten seconds, whilst continuing to observe the memory – represents the stomach meridian – where anxiety tends to reside.
4. Cup hands again around the ears ala TAT pose and re-check the image/memory to note what, if anything, has happened to that scene. If it has

cleared then great – if not then it suggests we need to use the Inner Child/Adult Self-Reclamation exercise for shock, as the scene is likely 'trapped and froze' and deeper work needs to be done.

All matter, even at the subatomic level, is formed of tiny drops of frozen light - a kind of focused mini-energy field, (ibid. p. 351) and according to Gerber, there are various quartz-like structures in the physical and subtle bodies that augment the impact of vibrational remedies. In the physical body, these areas include; cell salts, fatty tissue, lymphs red and white cells, and the pineal gland. (ibid. p. 344) The recognition of a crystalline substance being located within the pineal gland (third eye) allows for an understanding as to why tapping that point can have such an impact on a "frozen image". I often suggest to clients that when a traumatic scene appears frozen in their "mind's eye", they just tap the bridge of the nose/beginning of the eyebrow point. After a while the image usually starts to move again, and the client should be able to follow the incident to its completion, with the full awareness of all "parts" that they have indeed survived. The crystalline storage structure in the pineal gland may also be important to psychic receptivity, but its benefits could be stunted by some form of pineal calcification, which in turn could stop the natural process of relevant emotions as well as the pineal's production of melatonin.

In their natural ability to accept and hold a healing thoughtform, crystals are similar to magnetic recording media like the floppy disk. The life-force works through the blood and consciousness works more through the brain and nervous system. These two systems both have quartz-like properties and an electromagnetic current. The gem elixir, because of its resonant effect on the crystalline structures of the pineal gland and spinal cord, which are intimately involved in the kundalini process, seems able to enhance the practice of meditation and to assist the individual in achieving greater spiritual illumination. The right hemisphere seems to be attuned to the higher dimensional fields of consciousness of the Higher Self because the right brain has unique crystalline connections to the pineal gland.

(ibid. pps. 343-346)

Mel Kazinoff wrote about what he calls Monopoles and Melanin. Monopoles being microscopic cells within living organisms, acting as the interface between our outer world and our inner essence. Melanin being a complex chemical within us that seems to have the unique ability to self-create and which forms a microscopic crystal. This crystal is said to contain the memory of a resisted event in its entirety. He states that, "If we could access the memories contained in the melanin protein complex crystals and if we could then re-experience the memories without resistance, the crystal would dissolve and that resistance would be released." (Issues magazine - June/July 2002 pps. 32-33)

Great credit must be given to Tapas Fleming for developing the TAT method. She later added to this by including acupuncture points at the back of the head (where the brain`s vision center is located) and noted even further improvements.

Tapas Fleming`s own theory behind TAT is that a trauma is a stuck or frozen moment that continues to cause stress to the system, with some part of the victim trying to operate as though it never happened, based upon an inner belief that, "I can`t survive if this happens to me." This will then create a duality, or a yin-yang imbalance, as it would be called in Traditional Chinese Medicine. With TAT, you are consciously and deliberately reviewing the original "trauma scene", and acupressure is being performed to points that focus energy on the eyes, and it would appear to allow or confront the part(s) of oneself that rejected the trauma, doing so as a tool for surviving its origin. It stops being a threat and there tends to be subtle energy shifts and perceptual shifts that dissolve the duality and allows the system to relax, process and heal.

Some explanation of the relevance of the TAT pose (originated by Jane Wakefield) and the Three-Spot Tapping Points are provided below.

Interestingly, the points around the outside of the ears that the fingers press into are numbers 17-21 of the Triple Warmer meridian.

Bridge of nose, beginning of eyebrow = (Urinary Bladder – Fear, Restlessness and Trauma). Headaches, bronchial asthma, stomach cramps, fatigue, rheumatic diseases, skin diseases. Glandular imbalances, irritability, depression, and confusion. Stimulates immune functioning and calms the spirit.

The "Positive Points" (on the forehead, just above the eyes) bring energy and attention to the frontal lobes where rational thought is available without negative emotional overlay. Research into the integration of laser and holographic technologies for storing information has been ongoing by both Philips Research Labs of Hamburg, Germany and at Oak Ridge National Labs in Tennessee. There now exists the possibility of storing thousands of three-dimentional images in a single crystal. Crystals are used to create tiny lasers as well as light emitting diodes (LEDs), and in addition, biologists have come to recognize that many of the cellular membranes and structures in our bodies are also liquid crystals. (Gerber)

All matter, even at the subatomic level, is formed of tiny drops of frozen light - a kind of focused mini-energy field, and according to Gerber, there are various quartz-like structures in the physical and subtle bodies that augment the impact of vibrational remedies. In the physical body, these areas include; cell salts, fatty tissue, lymphs red and white cells, and the **pineal gland**. The recognition of a crystalline substance being located within the pineal gland (third eye) allows for an understanding as to why tapping that point can have such an impact on a "frozen image". I often suggest to clients that, when a traumatic scene appears frozen in their "mind's eye", they just tap the bridge of the nose/beginning of the eyebrow point. After a while the image usually starts to move again, and the client should be able to follow the incident to its completion, with the full awareness of all "parts" that they have indeed survived.

Side of the eyes (Gall Bladder – Rage) When there is a combined feeling of "being mad and helpless", i.e. rage, then tapping the side of outer eye plus the collarbone (K-27's) can be helpful in lowering the intensity.

Under eyes (Stomach - Fear) - Restoring tranquility and peace of mind, impotence and frigidity. The Stomach Meridian has been used very successfully to desensitize a patient to a fearful situation.

The **Eyes** – Healing can be that one's sensory perceptions become one, with the whole Self now using the same filter. The eyes may have frozen filters because what the eyes say is happening is what the rest of the senses believe is their truth, and we know that a belief is not necessarily THE truth!

The eyes may freeze the image that they capture at the moment a trauma is believed to be imminent, and this can therefore mean trapped/frozen light particles! C. S. Jordan and T.T. Lenington demonstrated that intense images of negative childhood memories are accompanied by changes in heart rate, galvanic skin response, respiration, and *eye movement*. ('Physiological Correlates of Eidetic Imagery and Induced Anxiety'. *Journal of Mental Imagery*. No. 3, 1979, pps. 31-42)

The eyes are attached, via meridians, to the stomach and, when feeling stressed, clients will often speak about getting "knotted up" in that region. When tapping under the eyes you may often hear and see the client sighing. This is most often a sign that a wave packet of energy has just been released and the client relieved of the "weight" of that energy they were carrying within them.

The eye registers the stimulations of light waves, while it is insensitive to sound. (Korzybski p. 235) When light enters the eyes, it first goes to the hypothalamus – the gland referred to in medicine as the brain's brain - since it not only regulates the body's life-sustaining functions, but also acts as a collecting station for all the information gathered by our senses and our psyche. Dr. Jacob Liberman feels that our openness to light has a direct correlation with our receptivity to things and situations in our lives.

The author demonstrating the recommended TAT pose
as modified by Jane Wakefield

The THREE-SPOT TAPPING POINTS

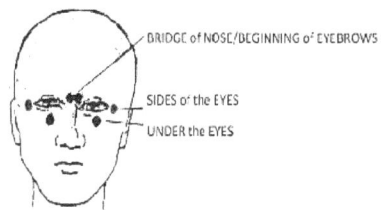

BRIDGE of NOSE/BEGINNING of EYEBROWS

SIDES of the EYES

UNDER the EYES

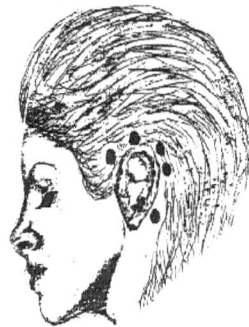

The additional position for Jane Wakefield's version of TAT,
with the hands cupped around the ears covering the pressure points as shown

CHAPTER ELEVEN

The Inner Child and Adult Self-Reclamation Exercise

"Your gratitude has the power to shift energy from negative to positive. It changes the chemical balance in your body from toxic to healing. Discouragement and depression cannot survive a powerful dose of genuine gratitude." (G. Richard Rieger)

* It is worth noting that I have found the Inner Child Reclamation exercise to be even more powerful and effective while the client is in the TAT position (as shown above).

My own experience has been that serious past trauma has often "frozen" the Inner Child or Adult Self in the scene (original location) of the trauma - that this part of them is still operating without the full knowledge that they have indeed survived, have grown up, and are no longer trapped.

This exercise should be used when there is a trauma scene that is still disturbing and painful for the client and where the person still feels immobilized, stuck, or frozen in the scene -

and there has been a lack of any shift with any other therapy. When no shift is occurring in the image or the level of feelings, one should ask the client if, for them, it is as though they are looking through the eyes of the child/adult, or like they were watching the scene on TV (like a third party).

If it is like watching TV, then request that they allow themselves as they are today to step into the image, and ask that they use further inner dialog to let the child/adult know who they are, that they have survived, that it is the year ----
(e.g. 2016), that they have a right to breathe, no matter what has happened to or around them. Clearly state, "You did not die!" Then at a steady pace when it seems appropriate, say, "If you sense that some of this information is not believed by that part, or any parts of you, then ask every part of you to become fully aware of the adult body in which you presently reside. Trust yourself to do what you know the child needs in order to recognize who you are, e.g. give a hug, put an arm around the shoulder, hold the hand or just have your mere presence alongside them. Let the child/adult self know that they are loved by you unconditionally and that you are sorry that you had to abandon them at that time, but that it was necessary for survival, and that from this time on they will never be abandoned by you again. Let the child know that you

realize that at this time these are only words but that over time they will be able to see that your words and your actions are congruent. Let the child/adult self know that in the situation they are in they can now make things bigger or smaller, change colors etc. as it is a way of recognizing you can now control and take charge of your memory with your imagination."

Use inner dialogue about now being able to live with "present day wisdom", which includes having the ability to recognize the present level of safety and to make choices based on no longer being dependent on others in the same sense that one might have been at a younger age. It may be that the Inner Child/Adult Self needs to have the present adult self stay with them in that image in order to confront an abuser or check that other children are not stuck or trapped there. Then state, "As the adult you are now, trust yourself to take the child to a present place of safety inside your own heart. You can carry him/her, put an arm around his/her shoulders, hold hands, or just have your mere presence alongside him/her. Remember that it is your image and you can command anything, or anyone, to leave or be present, including toys, sounds, sunshine, pictures etc." Once in this present place of safety the adult self should re-affirm to the Inner Child that, "From this time on, you will be able to communicate with the adult self anything you choose to about any "unfinished business" via words, pictures, images, or dreams." "Let the I.C. know that the present adult self will attend to the `unfinished business` at a pace that is safe and healthy, as and when it is appropriate to do so."

It is through this acknowledgement and action that the Inner Child/Adult Self will be able to shift the beliefs/paradigm with which they have been `frozen` for so long. Once the client indicates the child is safely with them, then suggest that the client`s adult self says goodbye to the Inner Child in a comforting and safe way, with reassurances that contact can be made anytime the Inner Child or Adult Self needs to.

N.B. The client should then return to the "frozen image" and begin the Three-Spot Tapping sequence in order to now totally clean and clear the original scene and, in my experience, the dissolution of the image and accompanying feelings begins.

I also suggest that, at the completion of this, one should thank the Self for having the courage to re-visit this painful memory and take time to feel how good it feels to have it gone 'lightened-up, no longer being a heavy weight getting dragged along with you wherever you go. I have had many clients state that they feel as if they have run a marathon afterwards and feeling tired as all that stored energy (the balloon) has been released. I urge them to rest and sleep once home if they are able to safely do so.

Interestingly my own observations of addictions make me feel that the major reasons for addictive behavior are as a reaction to **T**emptation, **A**nxiety, and **P**leasure (TAP), which could also stand for **T**emptation and **A**nticipation of **P**leasure/**P**ain or even the **T**emptation and **A**nxiety of **P**leasure/**P**ain. Given that tapping is a big component of the technique, it's a fitting acronym.

What if there is the feeling, e.g. fear, but no clear image of what it is connected to. Then suggest that the client go to the place within them where that feeling resides, and "Ask that part of you that knows to provide you with an image of what that feeling would `look` like if it were to look like something". Ask them to trust whatever is presented to them and then to retain that image in the "mind`s eye". With two fingers either side of the bridge of the nose and the beginning of the eyebrows, tap with the pads of the fingers. This will often dissipate the image, and lessen the intensity of the feeling.

A disorder called the Charcot-Wibrand Syndrome refers to the generalized inability to conjure up visual images. The wide dispersion of brain areas involved in imagery, especially visual imagery - indicates the importance of imagery to the survival of the species. Normally, highly important abilities are protected by being redundantly stored, as in this case. (Achterberg p. 126) Sometimes you will find that a client does not have the capacity to `see` images. In this case their imagery may just consist of only colors such as black or red. Regardless, it is a good idea to focus on the color and tap either side of the bridge of the nose and beginning of the eyebrows - that will usually still "lighten up" the image and the body`s general wellbeing. Other may not be able to "tune-in" to feelings (alexythymia) relating to a particular trauma, and often the use of other techniques will remove the protective sheath so that the emotions can finally be processed.

CHAPTER TWELVE

Embrace the Now and Maintain the Momentum

"You cannot control what happens to you, but you can control your attitude toward what happens to you, and in that, you will be mastering change rather than allowing it to master you." (Brian Tracy)

The original goals were to clean and clear the energy packets/triggers – those compartmentalized, buried, swallowed, stuffed, painful memories and to become a healthy guardian, advocate, friend, steward, custodian of and to all 'parts' of the Self at and for all ages and stages of your life. To eliminate self-sabotage – to be healthily spontaneous and to be steering the boat again (for some it will be for the first time). It was also to move from being guided by fear, pain and fear of more pain into living fully in the present - to peace, tranquility, serenity and being available for the full palace of possibilities that exist in the now. Being authentically present and responsive – rather than stuck and reactive. Moving from addictions and artificial grace to a state of true gratefulness (grace and attitude of gratitude) – from being dis-spirited and possibly over-using spirits (alcohol) into embracing your spiritual nature.

Huna author, teacher and practitioner Serge King also points out that, "Critical analysis …is recognition and recommendation without judgement." (1990 p. 93) He also takes the view that "If ever a group of people could be said to follow a system of spiritual democracy, it would be the shamans of the world." (ibid. p. 19)

The Huna philosophy consists of seven basic principles:

1) The world is what you think it is.

2) There are no limits.

3) Energy flows where attention goes.

4) Now is the moment of power.

5) To love is to be happy with – love is the only ethic needed in Huna.

6) All power comes from within.

7) Effectiveness is the measure of truth.

The kahunas look at things in terms of energy flow, and as far as they are concerned an idea or belief can block energy flow as much as muscle tension can. They practice what is called "lomi-lomi", described as "bioenergetic massage". The work done by the practitioner also includes working on the mind of the client, but it is similar to Swedish or Esalen massage, acupressure, polarity therapy and positive mental programming. (King 1985, p. 92) They refer to working on and releasing "complexes", which could be seen as similar to the COEX packets that were described by Stanislav Grof. The practice of *lomi lomi* is part of what the hunas call *kala*, and apart from the bodywork they also focus on clearing the mind of guilt and resentments, and forgiveness of self and others. As we can embrace philosophies such as Huna, the Hawaiians also utilise Ho'oponopono, as a means of healing, to 'clean and clear', to experience life without triggers or 'frozen' energy, to let go/forgive and restore. It has many similarities to Restorative Justice and Truth and Reconciliation. The most well-known practitioner and modern day guide to this would be Dr. Hew Len Ihaleakala, who was mostly brought to the world's attention by author Joe Vitale in his co-written book *'Zero Limits'*.

The Ho'oponopono Prayer below is an example of wanting to no longer carrying any old 'weight' around, like a sack of coals that would just get heavier over time.

"Divine Creator, Father, Mother, Son as One.

If I, my family, relatives or ancestors have offended you, your family, relatives, and ancestors in thoughts, words, deeds or actions - from the beginning of our creation to the present, we ask for forgiveness.

Let this cleanse, purify, release, cut all the negative memories, blocks, energies or vibrations, and transmute these unwanted energies to pure light. And it is done."

If interested in further TFT/EFT tapping work then I would recommend that you check out Nick Ortner's online World Tapping summit and Gary Craig's EFT and Optimal EFT websites. Both also have free, regular online newsletters.

Collapsing and Dissipating = Closure = Freedom.
Maintenance = grounding in today and in good health.

Yesterday will no longer determine how tomorrow will be!

Some recommended reading on the subjects herein:

Richard Gerber '*Vibrational Medicine*'
Johann Hari '*Chasing the Scream*'
Bruce Lipton '*The Biology of Belief*'
Serge King (no relation) '*Mastering your Hidden Self*'
Stephen P. King '*Rapid Recovery: Accelerated Information Processing & Healing*'
Gabor Mate '*In the Realm of the Hungry Ghosts*'
Eckhart Tolle '*The Power of Now*'
William Wittmann – an article entitled '*Amazingly Content*'
www.BodyAndSoulMentor.com

CHAPTER THIRTEEN

Summary

"An enthusiastic heart finds opportunities everywhere." Paulo Coelho

So – let's sum up the order in which I suggest you work through or assist clients in working through PTSD and release the impacts of shock and trauma – in finding freedom.

N.B. - It is vitally important to be able to breathe properly, but knowing that stress tends to lead us into holding our breath and tightening our chests, it is understandable if constricted breathing has become a habit for many of our overly-stressed clients. If you notice a client holding their breath please gently remind them to breathe, i.e. simply state "Please give yourself permission to breathe fully and deeply" You might even ask that they remind their self that they are presently safe and can open their eyes at any time they wish to in order to remind them of where they are right now – no longer stuck or trapped in a time or place.

Here is the recommended sequence:

1. Identify the triggers, traumas, energy packets and write/note the 'Trauma Time-Line List' (List ages and incidents and note the image(s) that go with them.

2. Drink water for hydration.

3. Do ND Correction i.e. Collarbone Breathing.

4. Use Inner Dialogue and remind the Self of surviving and how things are today.

5. Use the Simplest Technique on the trauma/shock scene first, i.e. the TAT pose and Three-Spot Tapping Process, while breathing fully and deeply.

6. If the imagery is still stuck or frozen – use the Inner Child/Adult Self-Reclamation technique.

7. Once out of the scene and safe in a present, loving place within your heart – put your attention back on the original image and tap as per Three-Spot Tapping locations until the scene has dissipated, disintegrated, moved off into the universal ether.

Through this graduated cleaning, clearing, collapsing and dissipating of traumas there comes closure, freedom and healthy spontaneity – a person becomes grounded in today and the newly authentic self emerges.

I hope that this has been helpful to you and that you can move on from any painful image or memory and live in an enlightened state, be fully present and be the authentic Self. I hope that you have broken negative repetitions, routines, rituals and reactions and can leave the turmoil of trauma to the history books.

Thank you for having the courage to 'care-front' yourself by taking these steps - and for humoring me!
I urge you to remain open to other energy psychology modalities and healing tools and techniques.

"Compassion is the barometer of grace."

N.B. If you would like to watch a preview of Steve King's companion PTSD online video course, go to
https://www.udemy.com/post-traumatic-stress-disorder/?instructorPreviewMode=guest

BIBLIOGRAPHY & REFERENCES

Achterberg, Jeanne. Imagery in Healing: Shamanism & Modern Medicine. Boston: New Science Library. Shambala. 1985.

Ballentine, Rudolph. Diet & Nutrition: a holistic approach. Honesdale, PA: Himalayan International Institute. 1978.

Ballentine, Rudolph. Radical Healing. New York: Harmony Books. 1999.

Barr, H.S. Blueprint for Immortality: The electric patterns of life. London: Neville Spearman. 1972.

Becker, Robert 0. & Selden, Gary. The Body Electric: Electromagnetism and the Foundation of Life. New York; Quill – William Morrow. 1985.

Blaisch, Robert 0. Applied Kinesiology and Human Performance. Selected papers. Int. College of Applied Kinesiology, pp 1-15, Winter, 1988.

Bohm, D. Wholeness and the Implicate Order. Boston: ARK Paperbacks. 1983.

Borysenko, Joan & Miroslav. The Power of the Mind to Heal. Carson, CA; Hay House Inc., 1994.

Brennan, Barbara Ann. Hands of Light: A guide to healing through the human energy field. New York: Bantam Books. 1987.

Callahan, Roger. Five Minute Phobia Cure. Wilmington, DE: Enterprise Publishing Inc., 1985.

Callahan, Roger. Why Do I Eat When I'm Not Hungry. New York: Doubleday. 1991

Campbell, Anthony. ed., Natural Health Handbook: A lifestyle guide to the principles and practice of alternative medicine. Sacaucus: NJ. Chartwell Books, Inc. 1984.

Clark, Hulda Regehr. The Cure for All Diseases. San Diego, CA: ProMotion Publishing, 1995.

Claude-Pierre, Peggy. The Secret Language of Eating Disorders. New York: Random House, Inc., 1997.

Craig, Gary and Fowlie, Adrienne. Emotional Freedom Techniques. The Manual. Second Edition. 1995 & 1997.

David-Neel, Alexandra. Magic and Mystery in Tibet. London: Abacus. 1977.

Dennison, Paul E, and Hargrove, Gail E. Personalised Whole Brain Integration. Glendale, CA: Edu-Kinesthetics Inc., 1985.

Diamond, John. Life Energy. New York: Dodd, Mead & Co., 1985.

Diamond, John. Your Body Doesn't Lie. New York: Warner Books, 1979.

Durlacher, James V. Freedom from Fear Forever. Tempe, AZ: Van Ness Publishing.1995.

Dyer, Dr. Wayne W. Your Sacred Self. New York: Harper Collins. 1995.

Eden, Donna with Feinstein, David. Energy Medicine. New York: Jeremy P.Tarcher. 1998.

Emerson, William R. & Schorr-Kon, Stephan. Innovative Therapies. Open University Press.1993.

Emerson, William R. Shock: A universal malady: Prenatal and peri-natal origins of suffering. Audiotape/booklet set. Petaluma, CA: Emerson Training Seminars. 1999.

Emoto, Masaru. Messages From Water. Tokyo, Japan: Hado Kyoikusha. 2001.

Enriquez, Juan. As the Future Catches You: How Genomics & Other Forces are Changing your Life, Work, Health & Wealth. New York: Crown Business. 2001.

Ferguson, Marilyn. The Aquarian Conspiracy: Personal and Social Transformation in Our Time. Los Angeles, CA: J.P. Tarcher, Inc. 1980.

Ferguson, Marilyn, Perrin, Patricia and Coleman, William S.E. Pragmagic. New York: Pocket Books, 1990.

Fleming, Tapas. Reduce Traumatic Stress in Minutes – The Tapas Acupressure Technique (TAT) Workbook. 5031 Pacific Coast Hwy. #76, Torrance, CA 90505.

Frankl, Viktor E. Man's Search For Meaning. New York: Washington Square Press. 1985.

Gach, Michael Reed. Acupressure's Potent Points: A Guide to Self-Care for Common Ailments. New York: Bantam Books. 1990.

Gerber, Richard. Vibrational Medicine. Santa Fe, NM: Bear & Co. 1988.

Giscard d'Estaing, Valerie-Anne and Young, Mark. eds. Inventions and Discoveries 1993: What's Happened, What's Coming, What's That? New York: Facts on File, Inc. 1993.

Goldman, Bob. with Patricia Bush and Ronald Klatz. Death In The Locker Room: Steroids, Cocaine & Sport. Tucson, AZ: The Body Press. 1984.

Goleman, Daniel. Emotional Intelligence. New York: Bantam Books. 1995

Goodheart, George J. Applied Kinesiology Research Manuals. Detroit; 1964-71.

Gottschalk Olsen, Kristin. The Encyclopedia of Alternative Health Care. New York: Pocket Books. 1990.

Gregory, Scott J. & Leonardo, Bianca. Conquering Aids Now: With natural treatment, a non-drug approach. Santa Monica, CA: Tree of Life Publications: 1986.

Grof, Stanislav with Bennett, Hal Zina. The Holotropic Mind. San Francisco, CA: Harper. 1993.

Hadeler, Hajo. Shiatsu for Two. Madeira Park, B.C.: Harbour Publishing. 1988.

Hawkins, David & Pauling, Linus.. eds., Orthomolecular Psychiatry: Treatment of Schizophrenia. San Francisco, CA: W. H. Freeman & Co. 1973.

Hawkins, David R. Power vs. Force: the Hidden Determinants of Human Behavior. Carlsbad, CA: Hay House, Inc. 2002.

Hills, Christopher. ed., Energy Matter & Form: Toward a Science of Consciousness. Boulder Creek, CA: University of the Trees Press. 1977.

Jacobi, Yolande, ed., Psychological Reflections: An Anthology of the Writings of C.G. Jung.New York: Harper & Row, 1961.

Janov, Arthur. The New Primal Scream: Primal Therapy 20 Years On. Wilmington, DE Enterprise Publishing Inc., 1991.

Janov, Arthur. Imprints: The Lifelong Effects of the Birth Experience. Toronto, ONT: General Publishing Co. 1983.

Jenny, Hans. Cymatics. Vol. 2. Basel, Switzerland: Bailius Presse AG. 1974.

Judith, Anodea and Vega, Selene. The Sevenfold Journey: Reclaiming Mind, Body & Spirit Through the Chakras. Freedom, CA: The Crossing Press. 1993.

Kaplan, Robert. Seeing Beyond 20/20. Hillsboro, OR: Beyond Words Publishing, Inc. 1987.

Kason, Yvonne. Farther Shores: Exploring How Near-Death Kundalini and Mystical Experiences Can Transform Ordinary Lives. Toronto, ONT: HarperCollins. 2000.

Keleman, Stanley. The Structure of Experience. Berkeley, CA: Center Press. 1985.

King, Serge. Earth Energies: A Quest for the Hidden Power of the Planet. Wheaton, Ill: Quest Books. 1992.

King, Serge. Mastering Your Hidden Self: A Guide to the Huna Way. Wheaton, Ill: Quest Books. 1985.

King, Serge. Urban Shaman. New York: Simon & Schuster. 1990.

Kreiger, Dolores. The Therapeutic Touch: How to use your hands to help or to heal. New York: Simon & Schuster. 1979.

Kreiger, Dolores. Accepting Your Power to Heal: The personal practice of Therapeutic Touch. Santa Fe, NM: Bear & Co. 1993.

Kopp, Sheldon. Here I Am, Wasn't I!: The Inevitable Disruption of Easy Times. New York: Bantam Books. 1986.

Korzybski, Alfred. Science and Sanity: An Introduction to Non-Aristotelian Systems and General Semantics. 4th Edition. Lakeville, Connecticut: The International Non-Aristotelian Library Publishing Co. 1958.

Larson, Joan Mathews, Sehnert, Keith W. Seven Weeks to Sobriety. New York, NY: Ballantine Wellspring. 1997.

Lendl, Jennifer & Foster, Sandra. EMDR 'Performance Enhancement' for the Workplace: a 'Practitioners' Manual. San Jose, CA: Performance Enhancement Unlimited. 1997.

Lepore, Donald. The Ultimate Healing System. Provo, Utah: Woodland Books. 1988.

Liberman, Jacob. Light: Medicine of the Future. Santa Fe, NM: Bear & Co. 1991.

Maltz, Maxwell. Psycho-Cybernetic Principles for Creative Living. Markham, ONT: Pocket Books. 1974.

Manning, Jeane. The Coming Energy Revolution. Garden City Park, NY: Avery 1996.

Millon, Theodore. Modern Psychopathology. Philadelphia: W.B. Saunders Co. 1969.

Mountrose, Phillip & Jane. Getting Thru to Your Emotions with EFT. Sacramento, CA: Holistic Communications. 2000.

Moyers, Bill. Healing and the Mind. New York: Doubleday. 1993.

Nickel, David J. Acupressure for Athletes. New York: Henry Holt & Co, Inc.1984.

Nordenstrom, B. Biologically Closed Electric Circuits: Clinical, experimental and theoretical evidence for an additional circulatory system.. Stockholm, Sweden: Nordic. 1983.

Paulson, Genevieve Lewis. Kundalini and the Chakras: A Practical Manual. St.Paul Minnesota: Llewellyn Publications, Inc. 1993.

Peck, M. Scott. The Road Less Traveled. New York: Simon and Schuster. 1978.

Pert, Candace B. Molecules of Emotion. New York: Touchstone. 1999.

Pribram, K.H. Languages of the Brain: Experimental paradoxes and principles in neuropsychology. New York: Brandon House. 1981.

Sahley, Billie Jay and Birkner, Katherine M. Breaking Your Addiction Habit. San Antonio, TX: Pain & Stress Therapy Center Publication. 1990.

Sahley, Billie Jay. The Anxiety Epidemic. San Antonio, TX: Pain & Stress Therapy Center Publication, 1994.

Sahley, Billie Jay. Control Hyperactivity with Amino Acids and Nutrient Therapy. San Antonio, TX: Pain & Stress Therapy Center Publications. 1994.

Sanella, Lee. The Kundalini Experience. Lower Lake, CA: Integral Publishing. 1987.

Shapiro, Francine. Eye Movement Desensitisation and Reprocessing: Basic Principles, Protocols and Procedures. New York: The Guilford Press. 1995.

Sheldrake, Rupert. A New Science of Life: The Hypothesis of Formative Causation. Los Angeles: Jeremy P. Tarcher, Inc. 1981.

Sheppard, Kay. Food Addiction: The Body Knows. Deerfield Beach, FL: Health Communications. 1989.

Siegel, Bernie S. Love, Medicine & Miracles. New York: Harper & Row. 1986.

Stokes, Gordon & Whiteside, Daniel. Tools of the Trade: for understanding & trusting our self. Burbank, CA: Thoth Inc. 1991.

Talbot, Michael. The Holographic Universe. New York: HarperCollins. 1991.

Takahashi, Masaru and Brown, Stephen. Qigong for Health: Chinese Traditional Exercise for Cure and Prevention. New York: Japan Publications, Inc.1986.

Teeguarden, Iona Marsaa. The Joy of Feeling. Tokyo: Japan Publications. 1987.

Thie, John F., with Marks, Mary. Touch for Health. Marina del Rey, CA: DeVorss & Co.1973

Ullman, Dana. Homeopathy: Medicine for the 21st Century. Berkeley, CA: North Atlantic Books. 1988.

Walther, David S. Applied Kinesiology. Vols. 1 and 2.
Abriendo, CO: Systems DC, 1981.

Weller, Charles, and Boylan, Brian Richard. How to Live
with Hypoglycemia. New York, NY Award Books. 1978.

Wharnock, John. Simply Living and Loving. Edmonton,
Alberta: Twin Dolphins Co., 1989

Whisenant, William F. Psychological Kinesiology: Changing
the Body's Beliefs. Kailua, HI: Monarch Butterfly
Productions, 1994.

Whitfield, Charles. Healing the Child Within. Deerfield
Beach, FL: Health Communications, Inc.1989.

Winterdyk, John, & Jensen, Karen. The Complete Athlete:
Integrating Fitness, Nutrition and Natural Health. Burnaby,
B.C.: Alive Books. 1997.

www.ingramcontent.com/pod-product-compliance
Lightning Source LLC
Chambersburg PA
CBHW081408270326
41931CB00016B/3418